IN DEFENSE OF RELIGION

JOHN GIBSON

In Defense of Religion

Published by Wheatmark®
610 East Delano Street, Suite 104
Tucson, Arizona 85705 U.S.A.
www.wheatmark.com

International Standard Book Number: 978-1-60494-083-1
Library of Congress Control Number: 2008920611

This book I dedicate to Lord Venkateshwara, also known as Lord Balaji, Lord Perumal, Lord Srinivasan, and Lord of the Seven Hills. When I say God I mean you if I mean someone definite, and when I say you I definitely mean God.

CONTENTS

FOREWORD

I'm writing for the many who'd be religious if religion hadn't been made to appear so repulsive by the enemies of all religion and the friends of bad religion.

Religion's reputation, not its reality, is what requires defending. This isn't a defensive defense, more an explanation of what religion is most rewardingly seen to be and of what's wrong with the assumptions and the reasoning and the instincts of its critics.

What's assayed here isn't theology. It doesn't say what God is or ask everyone to abide by a single theory of God or even by a belief in God. Nor is it answerable to any religion's authority. "Philosophy" is both too august a word and one I reverence too much for me to feel comfortable using it for what I'm about. That could be termed freelance polemicism, or just argumentativeness.

It appears to me that theologians and apologists and pastors and even scientists who are religious have been unsuccessful in deflecting rationalist attacks. Why? I think it's because they've felt obliged to argue for the factuality of their religions' beliefs, which they're unable to establish. I'm using another strategy, going by what religion does and therefore what it is.

The new rationalists are angry, militant, spoiling for a fight. Older-type rationalists aren't. By now the two may wish to be told apart. So I propose that the name "rationalists" apply to the newer sort, as they attract more notoriety and are identified in the public mind with it. For the older sort I propose "sciists" (SY-ists), sci being short for science.

Sciists have a bridge through their non-theism to spiritu-ally competent non-theists such as the Dalai Lama, who have a bridge through their spirituality to theists, so that in principle fruitful exchanges can take place among them all. Rationalists have no bridges that they don't blow up. Like fundamentalists, they acknowledge nothing that can serve as common ground with others.

Just as we've seen that fundamentalists can be power-hungry, we're seeing now that the same is true of rationalists. Both *de-mand* that everyone agree with them and itch to make life harder for those who won't.

That demand for agreement, once made, outpaces good will and reason. It pits egoism against the requirements of civiliza-tion.

If scientists were as doctrinaire about nature as rationalists are about religion, we'd still be looking for phlogiston.

As experiencing beings, we have in religion our largest con-text: one that's involving, moving, and engagingly mysterious, as well as able to change us. Evidence suggests it's able sometimes to change even our external circumstances in ways that are called miraculous. Rationalists find that idea abhorrent and infuriating. I find it marvelous.

Finally: I think we can appreciate religion better if it's recon-sidered and reconceptualized. A glossary is provided at the end of the book for new terminology, as I'm introducing some fifteen concepts as prisms for fresh seeing.

ONE

WHAT RELIGION IS

I

What historic figure do we see as the personification of reason? The likeliest might be Socrates, who's credited with bringing critical thinking into everyday life.

Those who believe that reason and religion are opposites might offer him as their symbol, perhaps with Jesus symbolizing religion. They could denominate the Athenian "Father of Rationalism."

Or maybe they'd better not. Consider this quote: "(W)hat evidence did they produce that Socrates refused to recognize the gods acknowledged by the state? Was it that he did not sacrifice? Or that he dispensed with divination? On the contrary, he was often to be seen engaged in sacrifice, at home or at the common altars of the state. Nor was his dependence on divination less manifest. Indeed that saying of his 'A divinity gives me a sign,' was on everybody's lips." (Xenophon, The Memorabilia, 2006, Objective Systems Pty Ltd., large type edition, pp.1-2)

Plato depicted Socrates' religiousness in a seemingly offhand way. Xenophon, who like Plato was his student and knew him well, reminded the people of Athens how pivotal religion had been in his life and work.

Socrates' religiousness can't be "excused" on the ground that it was a pre-scientific time. There were atheistic and scientifically-inclined persons in that period, including famous materialist philosophers like Anaxagoras, Democritus, Parmenides, and

Thales. Socrates wasn't unmindful of their reputations or their stances.

Rationalists, of course, would like to see him as without religion and against it. Likewise, many monotheists are repelled at the thought that such an outstanding individual could have worshiped pagan gods and so might prefer to imagine him an agnostic. But his religiousness crystallized who he was.

Socrates represents religion and reason together, each in full flower. Today this may satisfy neither side. But maybe that's what's wrong with how we think—or don't think—today.

Xenophon: "'The divinity,' he said, 'gives me a sign.' Further he would constantly advise his associates to do this, or beware of doing that, upon the authority of this same divine voice; and, as a matter of fact, those who listened to his warnings prospered, whilst he who turned a deaf ear to them repented afterwards." (p.3) What provides true information isn't reducible to superstition.

We know little of what occurred, so we have to take what we're told as what may have been rather than what was or what couldn't have been. And how different from most of what we hear about religion is what we hear about the religion of Socrates!

He was self-trained to challenge assumptions and uphold what holds up under scrutiny. The victims of his *elenchus* were those who refused to notice and listen and re-think and learn. He made examples of them for the instruction of his young friends and for the good of the community.

Xenophon: "(H)e was plainly a lover of the people, and indeed of all mankind." (p.46) "His formula or prayer was simple: 'Give me that which is best for me,' for, said he, the gods know best what good things are..." (p.50) He treasured "the consciousness of becoming better oneself..." (p.79) And "he was...eager to cultivate a spirit of independence in others, which would enable them to stand alone in all transactions suited to their powers." (p.433) Notice that: "a spirit of independence" and not one of dutiful conformity!

"Where any one came seeking for help which no human wisdom could supply, he would counsel him to give heed to 'divination.' He who has the secret of the means whereby the gods give signs to men touching their affairs can never surely find himself bereft of heavenly guidance." (p.441) Someone like this was religious in no casual or dissociated way.

Socrates was in some respects an original. But you can also see that some of his traits were representative of the best religious people, including his gratefulness, his humility, his invariable self-discipline, his cheerfulness, his simplicity, his desire to be of service, his courage, his generosity, his willing poverty and need of little, and his flat-out rejection of sensuality and the weaknesses and character deformations that it leads to. Today this "gadfly" would sting rationalists and fundamentalists, just as he stung the know-it-alls of his own time.

But what attracted people to him and held them in his orbit was not his forensic skill but a more perfectly rounded humanity that enticed or shamed them into trying to be like him. Read Xenophon or Plato and you can't miss that.

Socrates thought that both religion and reason should free you from loyalty to what's mistaken in you, *and* from having to have your own way.

It's revealing that he advised the young Xenophon to ask the Oracle at Delphi whether Xenophon should go abroad and meet Cyrus, as he had been invited to do. Wanting to make the journey, Xenophon asked not *whether* but *how* he should go. Socrates permitted his departure but disapproved of this evasion, which abused the application to the deity and let the applicant abide by his own inclination. (Diogenes Laertius, Lives of Eminent Philosophers, translated by R.D. Hicks, Harvard University Press, Cambridge, Massachusetts & London, 1972, pp.179-181)

His service to the civic and personal reclamation of the young men of Athens by engaging them in philosophy, and his trust in the gods, and his faithful performance of divination and prayer and sacrificial rites were components of a highly integrated religious life. Minus that, we'd never have heard of him.

If we today can't put questions to the Delphi Oracle, many

nevertheless say we can receive intimations by wanting them, being alert for them, and humbling and disciplining ourselves. That comes down to a thesis that we may be able to substantiate.

People of the sort who regard it as discrediting of religion that we no longer believe in the gods Socrates worshiped are locked into the irrelevant. What we know of gods or God—and Socrates used both expressions—is what happens to us in relation to them.

The great traditions and the great mystics have told us that what's beyond ourselves is ineffable. If no description is adequate to it, then what we believe about it is meaningful primarily as it sensitizes us to it, not in portraying it to our intellects. Insofar, worship is instrumental and not a mark of ignorance.

II

Religion calls for and calls forth relinquishment. It's forgiveness in Christianity, submission in Islam, liberation in the Eastern traditions, always a releasing of something for the sake of something else. For Socrates relinquishment meant adjusting his course with alacrity as reason or the Oracle or the inner deity instructed.

It's the sending off of all that you are and have and want, the best as well as the worst, including your convictions and theories, to God or to gods or "to whom it may concern." What you get back may be—should be—a better version of it in a freer person.

Religious application can revolutionize what you're able to feel, detect, bear, adapt to, resist, appreciate, effect, affect, and be. It does so best when you're best able to let it do so completely. Or is that mistaken? I should think we'd make a bid to know.

Here's a metaphor for it. Writing a book, I've found, makes for seemingly endless revising, from full reorganization to the deft substitution of a lone word. What's best in the text tests the quality and relevance of everything else in it. Then it's tested in turn, as an upgrade in one location calls for upgrades elsewhere and eventually everywhere. So it is with the revising of a person.

To be revised is to be readied, and not for something but for anything.

The major religions provide undertakings for the sake of undergoings. All of them encourage us toward the surpassing of what we think of as the human condition, as did Socrates.

Religious belief doesn't consist in having beliefs. It's unlike belief in a proposition, which closes alternative avenues. It's the belief displayed when my believing *you* makes me receptive to what you say, or my believing *in* you makes me responsive to what you aspire to do.

To believe religiously, then, is to admit an influence into your life. The influence may or may not be ascribable to a deity.

Belief becomes reverence. Reverence becomes devotion. Devotion becomes concentration. Concentration becomes absorption.

Devotion is dedicated love. Religious devotion may be to a personage such as a god, or to a practice such as meditation, or to a goal such as Samadhi or Nirvana. What you're devoted to is the sounded note that your life reverberates to.

Devotedness introduces fearlessness into you. This happens through emotional identification with an ideality that you find more engaging than what's alluring in the world and more commanding of your heed than what's threatening.

Because devotedness brings fearlessness, it brings clarity. When you have it, you can look upon anything and be willing to see and accept it as it is. It's a subjectivity that facilitates objectivity in you. Socrates knew this well.

I'd say that if you're fearlessly intelligent, you can deal appropriately, dispassionately, skillfully, ruthlessly when necessary, with even the most trying conditions. For this reason true religion is advantageous to a scientist.

By intelligence I mean percipiency, creativity, imaginativeness, efficiency, far-sightedness, intuitiveness, and what's of near kin to them.

Wisdom is the most rounded practical intelligence. It entails immediate recognition of the ways of nature and of how to navigate in any situation, appearing to obviate the intermediary process of learning. It's the height of adaptation to life. According to witnesses it can include unexplained knowledge of facts.

Wisdom should therefore be of distinct interest to science, though it hasn't been. Scientists could approach agreed-upon persons of wisdom and observe what it is and how it's won.

A rendezvous between true science and true religion must sooner or later take place, especially as the conflict between distorted religion and distorted science keeps intensifying.

Religion's intellectual foes call themselves rationalists. They regard religious behavior as merely instinctual: as wishful thinking and denial, hence as incompatible with being intelligent. But in true religion there's unreservedly intelligent behavior. Do you doubt it? Consider a while whether it's not so.

Rationalists profess to be proponents of science and reason and opponents of "faith," by which they mean unprovable or unproven beliefs. Their own beliefs are at best unprovable, as they have no way of showing that they're justified in terming false all that's classified as "supernatural," which includes the paranormal, the religious, and the miraculous.

They do that in part to combat unscientific and anti-scientific interference with science, such as the fundamentalist attempt to neutralize facts with Bible verses. They do it also, however, as a strategy for making the world more manageable by seeing it as simpler than the totality of the evidence indicates it to be.

This amounts to inventing impossibilities, denying from the outset that some things are possible. It invalidates rationalism's claim to be scientific, as it's anti-empirical.

Some may hurry through this chapter saying, "Where's the proof?" It's permitted me to lay out what we're to take up before having to prove anything about it.

We have to get enough of a sense of religion to be able to vary our hypotheses about it and not merely reject them if our early tests come back negative. That's what we do if we want to know. Rationalists, by contrast, welcome any rationale for abandoning what's being asked after that goes against what they want to believe.

The second chapter will deal with how to investigate religion. Those who wish to can betake themselves there before reading what comes next and can use the glossary to catch up on the vocabulary that's introduced in the pages between here and there.

III

By "religion" I mean what the major religions embody in common, leaving aside what distinguishes each from any or all.

What have the religions in common, then? At least this: a self-giving-over, an experience of renewal or rescue, a mood of adoration toward something, a compassionate regard for all who are, a changeover of one's qualities, and some form of contemplative or meditative or devotional or internally discriminative practice.

Today religion is gaining the ascendancy over religions. This is happening because of immigration, studies in comparative religion, and rationalistic attacks on all religions as intolerable.

The ascendancy of religion won't cause religions to fade away but will affect how the people in them regard their own and those of their near and far neighbors.

That promises that not what religions say but what religion says will be decisive in the future.

Nothing can so weaken the repute of religion as religions. Nothing can so strengthen the repute of religions as religion.

In writing of "religion" I don't refer to a new, comprehensive religion intended to displace the current ones. Religion lets each religion remain, and remain what it is. But it understands any relative to all.

The differences among religions when at their best are more like the differences among flavors of ice cream than like, say, the difference between a dream and sand.

Religious disagreements, even over such a divisive issue as theism, don't weaken religion or divide people who are truly-religious. Religions agree on what's of primary practical importance: that we ourselves can come to be autonomous, wise, unafraid, beneficent, and available to higher experiencing. As the promise of all the major religions, that's the promise of religion.

The defects and deficiencies that befall the religions over time can be remedied as the people within one reflect on what's rightest in the rest. As Sri Sri Ravi Shankar has advised, all traditions can belong to each of us, rather than each of us belonging to but a single one of them. Such a trend can produce religious unity by leaving us with no reason for invidious thinking.

In a world in which multiple religions are becoming known to the multiplying multitude who are educated, all of us on earth will one day be able to select one through affinity. If you can choose a spouse, a location, a career, why shouldn't you choose for yourself among religions rather than go by how your ancestors worshiped or what those around you believe?

If you can try on a hat, why can't you try on a religion? If you have a hat that fits you, why can't you have a religion that fits you? If you own a reversible hat, why can't you incorporate into your religion what you like best from several religions? And do you blame other people for wearing hats in sizes that aren't the same as yours?

This'll be denounced as "relativism" by those who want absolutism. Absolutism makes us tyrannical and unable to admit error; relativism makes us beliefless, undiscriminating, and indifferent. Relativism by itself and absolutism by itself are destructive; it's only when they're fitted together adeptly that we intelligently balance freedom and truth so as not to lose either.

Whoever argues against religion on behalf of some religion will lose the argument. If anything could hurt religion, it'd also hurt the religion that was argued for.

(A few years ago I attended services several times at a United Methodist church where the congregants were friendly and the atmosphere was relaxed and warm. I think it curious that what they officially profess somewhat belies that openness, when it could be as generous and welcoming as the people themselves are without being mindlessly eclectic or complacent about wrongs.)

The day may come, I suggest, when most places of worship will incorporate counsel, tales, holy persons, and practices from several traditions.

I don't mean to imply that there'll be a general and permanent synthesis of some or all religions; their distinctive attributes in varying and shifting combinations and the element of choice that those represent have abiding value for participation.

Nor do I think that the combinations wrought must water down each religion. Intelligently planned, the included religions can be concentrated and sharpened, rather than dulled and diluted, as we compare and contrast them.

It isn't difficult to picture a house of worship with separate stained glass windows that depict Jesus and the Buddha and Krishna, and with lectures and written material that present them and Muhammad and other religious figures in depth and independently of one another. (There has been a modest start to this in some places; the Riverside Church in Manhattan, which is interdenominational Protestant, has displays which honor Muhammad as well as secular contributors to our lives such as Einstein and Pasteur.)

Attune yourself to the greats of the various religions one at a time, and I predict you won't find the experience of any to deplete that of another.

I don't forecast that such institutions will be along speedily, just that they'll be along. We've been heading in that direction for generations.

Any of the major traditions, employed in the right spirit and with the right effort, will avail us, as we can gather by viewing the most adoring and adorable worshipers in each.

Rationalists can challenge the beliefs of a religion—whether Jesus rose from the dead, whether Adam and Eve were our ancestors, whether Brahma created the world, etc.—if those are taken to be factual. (I'll have more to say below about that qualification.) But to critique religion, as opposed to religions, is a task of another magnitude. From the standpoint of religion, the religions' vulnerable assertions are merely instantiations of principles.

For example, when Christians say that to receive grace is possible only through belief in Jesus Christ as savior, this can't be proved and furthermore can be disproved by observing the best of in the other traditions. From the standpoint of religion, then, such a statement dramatizes, and doesn't exhaust, the principle that it exemplifies: that devotion (of some type) is the way past our faults and the low-mindedness, pessimism, and cynicism that can lead to rationalism or despondency or immersion in decadence.

Because it's evil when met head-on, the exclusivistic has to be appropriated wisely. Let it bestow on us pictures, not theses. It's representative and mustn't be taken on its own terms, else we be obliged to prove what has no proof and end by doing violence to one another and ourselves.

Religion isn't tied to religions' specifics. To it, religions are cases-in-point from a cluster of desiderata. It has not beliefs but themes. The utterances heeded in it don't define but exemplify. Its concern is not with *a religion's* doctrines or historicity but with *our* higher possibilities.

That goes for Western religion, for Eastern religion, and for bygone religions like that of Socrates.

Religion over religions is departicularization: the overcoming of our enclosedness in particular particulars. It dispenses with their indispensability. This makes possible a universalization of outlook.

To achieve universalization and leave behind partiality in its supposed necessity is to be intelligent over-all.

IV

Among religious persons we find more than a few who are good, a few who are very good, and a very few who are more than good.

If some lives can be outstanding, why can't many more? And if those who are outstanding are the happiest and least conflicted among us, as they may believably be, what prevents our being like them? Through traditional or newfound methods, might we come to be more as they are?

What better could science do for us than to follow through on such questions?

For nothing guarantees that our physical circumstances can be made agreeable. To be free within, even when unfree without, is requisite if we aren't to suffer avoidably. It's what must occur if one is to fully own oneself and not be mentally scattered and disheartened by life's vicissitudes.

To own oneself might strike some as contradictory of relinquishing oneself. But how far can one give away what one hasn't laid claim to and doesn't truly possess? And the only way to possess it is to be willing to give it away!

Self-owning is one facet of existence at its best. By purposing in a relaxed way, you can reclaim from the world all of your tendrils and projections. You can submit them for revising and be emotionally prepared to receive them back purified and elevated, or to receive something in their stead. That's to be freer.

Religions have told us different procedures for achieving interior freedom. Scientists may be able to identify more and make some accessible to everyone. But first they have to ask about it. In today's culture there's a double prohibition, from both rationalism and fundamentalism, against their doing so.

Religion's besetting malady is fundamentalism. Science's besetting malady is rationalism.

To rationalists, religion is bad science. To fundamentalists, science is bad religion. (To everyone else, fundamentalism is bad religion and rationalism is bad science.)

Science conducts research with scientific method. You could say it's curiosity with a few rules. True science is the willingness to search out the truth of things and let it be whatever it is: even if what it turns out to be displeases some or all of us.

Fundamentalism I'll define as the view that some specified

religion's scriptures, stories, and beliefs are necessarily of a factual character and flawlessly accurate.

Religion I'll define as *beyonding*. To beyond is to relate oneself
to what one conceives to exceed the psychological and material
bounds we're all familiar with in the interest of one's being made
more satisfactory. It's our approach, effective or not, to whatever
might take us to God or gods or some *supernal* way of being.

True religion is constituted by what we do to develop in ourselves devotion and high characteristics such as vision, intuitiveness, fearlessness, purity, wisdom, and compassion.

It can be observed that the beliefs of rationalism shut down
our scientific and personal curiosity about the paranormal, the
otherworldly, the sacred, deities, the miraculous, an afterlife, and
all else that's "supernatural."

(I'm putting the phrases "the supernatural" and "the laws of
nature" in quotes, because they contain debatable assumptions.
It's not self-evident that science's laws are more than generaliz-
ations or that anything, including God, is other than natural.
I don't put the word paranormal in quotes because I see it as
straightforward: the paranormal is what we don't normally run
up against.)

Our innate tendency is to acknowledge "the supernatural"
with pleasure and lively interest. To deny out of hand that it exists imposes an artificial restraint on our desire and capacity for
beyonding. And beyonding may be what's definitively human, in
the sense that to be fully human we must be willing to be more
than only human.

Rationalists overleap evidence with conclusions and not
merely hypotheses about how things are, as when they insist that
"the laws of nature" can't fail to be in force without exception.
For all to concur, they'd have to inform us *why* that must be so.

Following the examples of Charles Fort and William Corliss,
Forteans and other anomalists have for a century taken pains
to compile and publicize incidents that appear to violate "the
laws of nature." Paranormalists have been at work for a century
and a half looking into "supernatural" phenomena and are nowa-

days doing so with different kinds of electronic equipment that compensate for the unreliability of our senses. Scientists should examine these researchers' reports impartially and rigorously and find the laws, if there are any, behind the presumptive lawlessness.

And if there are none? Then there are none. It may appear simply obvious that causality and lawfulness must underlie phenomena. But all of us should realize that there's no way of knowing whether it's so. (David Hume, who borrowed his analysis from the early Buddhists, could find only "constant conjunction" in these regularities. How requisite causality or lawfulness can be, if it's only constant conjunction, is *not* obvious.)

The roles of law and cause are for evidence to determine.

"Learn to listen," the Zen poet Basho advised, "while things speak for themselves." That's to adjust our views as far as the evidence warrants.

If you were to show rationalists something miraculous they'd be made very uncomfortable unless they could explain it away. But why? True scientists would find it neutrally interesting and are at all times set to amend their views.

Rationalists excuse themselves by saying they want to get rid of all the nonsense so science can do its work. It's they who keep science from doing its most consequential work: engaging the highest and most remarkable things known and learning the ways they can be most relevant to ourselves.

Entire absence of such prejudice is what the East calls "enlightenment." What the West calls "The Enlightenment" began in the spirit of enlightenment to liberate the sciences from imprisonment within Christian doctrines. But it has issued in something unenlightened: in immutable prejudice against religion and "the supernatural."

It'll be said that the anomalous is too amorphous for scientists, too elusive for their methods, too distasteful to their proud hard-headedness. If scientists can track something as nebulous as a subatomic particle, they can come up with ways of taking on an alleged spirit or miracle that leaves behind material evidence.

And they may be able even to scan whatever the source is from which such mysterious entities come to us. What they can do has no foretellable limit.

Some will think what I'm saying here naïve. I'd ask them to hold off on that judgment till they've read further. Again I commend to you the next chapter, which considers the paranormal and science before it takes up science and religion.

V

The central claim of rationalists is one that ought to astound everyone. It's that they know what *can't* be. It's an opinion devoid of scientific merit. There's no way of saying that something couldn't exist. What has no existence is a matter of conjecture and won't be more than that unless our ways of knowing are augmented by something presently unforeseen. And the unforeseen is what rationalists *aren't* in quest of!

The method of science is concerned with ruling out possibilities, falsifying theories; but because we're prone to mistakes, scientific thinking is provisional, always prepared to reconsider if things don't "add up" in every respect. So while science is oriented first to impossibility, it pairs that with an orientation to possibility through its provisionality and the unendingness of its adjustments and its questioning. There's a balance in science which is lacking in rationalism.

True science and true religion go forward in their quests, incrementally or by leaps, implicitly disposed to do so indefinitely. I'll call that *infinintention* (in-fin-in-TEN-shun), the intention to "go infinite" and never rest.

Infinintention is a word that combines into one the thoughts "open-mindedness," "intelligence," "self-assurance," "tentativeness," and "humility." Infinintention is the attitude of the best religious and the best scientific minds.

It evokes humility with the recognition that we don't know everything. It evokes tentativeness with the recognition that the new will affect what we think about the old. It evokes self-assurance with the recognition that we have the strength to cheerfully tolerate indecision and ambiguity and needn't be shaken by them. It evokes intelligence with the recognition that we must notice and absorb subtle distinctions and what might disprove our theories. It evokes open-mindedness with the recognition that true devotion and true dedication don't disable but enable our adaptability.

By contrast, rationalists are committed to terminating the questions, closing off possibilities once and for all, so what they deem definitive knowledge can be had and anything disagreeable to their paradigm be dismissed straightaway.

These are two very different basic attitudes toward religion and science and life.

True religion is infinintentional through one's self-negation and readiness for everything that comes of it. True science is infinintentional through its systematic refusal to concede pre-set limits to what it can know, do, or be, and through its attentiveness to the unexpected and exceptions.

To be infinintent is a brave course. Intellectually it's a select one.

Infinintention is preparedness for the evolution of our knowing, understanding, and experiencing, even for the entire overthrow of all of those as they now are; that's how it connects to faith as trust.

If it's asked how infinintention is congruent with religious devotion—*I.e.* how one can be devoted to something yet prepared to release it for something else—the answer is that the commitment is to the attainable, not to the attained. If you should be referred, from what you're devoted to, to something greater, or if what you're devoted to should be revealed as greater than you had envisioned, how could that be other than a boon to you?

Our only way of distinguishing between what a situation that we've conceptualized really is and what we presently believe it to be is through the acknowledgement that our knowledge of it can be improved. (This takes us to Berkeley's "To be is to be perceived"; Kant's "thing-in-itself"; Hegel's dictum about the rational being the actual and the actual the rational; the indeterminacy of physics as discovered by Heisenberg; the relativity of the phenomenal as discovered by Einstein; the bafflingly true-yet-false character of relativism and perspectivism; and the liar paradox: "This statement is false," which is if false true and if true false. It may be that all of this exhibits a fundamental illusoriness in finite existence which the East refers to as "maya.") One thing should be clear: our knowledge can in principle never be fully adequate, our conceptualization never identical to the reality, which means that tentativeness is necessary and that infinintention is the engine of cognitive progress.

If so, then what isn't necessary or even sustainable is the identification of reality with impossibilities, which is rationalism's stock-in-trade.

The present spate of furious and dogmatic rationalist writings for the public may be the flare-up before the fire dies. Two things have already begun to kill rationalism. One is the increasing publication of the actual "impossible" experiences of numerous people, such as you'll find in this book, which decent and honest persons of science will have to take into account. Previously all of that was dismissed as a "fringe" thing; but there's too much of it now, and the people involved are too normal, too educated, and too culturally mainstream for it to be shrugged off. The other thing is the work of physicists, which is moving away from the rationalist model with informed speculation about many universes and dimensions as well as discoveries that are more and more incongruous to conventional minds. Rationalism is a drag in physics because it cripples the imagination and makes thought legalistic and fearful.

Also working against a general acceptance of rationalism is the unwillingness of religious people at every social level to be dissuaded by rationalists' hysterical and skewed characterizations of them.

Most who are religious respect those who differ with them. They realize that their worship has made them more kindly, helpful, high-minded, inwardly secure, and fit to raise children who are caring, self-disciplined, and emotionally mature. Nor are they less able than rationalists are to make calm, circumspect, and defensible decisions.

The bloody historical wrongs done for religions are more visible, but not therefore more typical or more important, than religion's countless good, constructive, unselfish lives with their countless telling acts of beneficence and moral courage.

Rationalists identify religion with superstition. True religion and true science are empirical, going by experience, and so aren't superstitious.

We have true science when we "hear things out" and don't pretend that we already know what they'll "say." We have rationalism when the existence of anything more commanding of reverence than our analytical minds is discounted in advance. We have fundamentalism when a single religion is taken without valid proof to be unqualifiedly authoritative. We have true religion when we unreservedly long to be with all that surpasses and gives rise to the best in us. Each of these pays off in its own coin.

Rationalism is an ideology. By an ideology I mean any version of how things are over-all that's preferred to discovery of how they genuinely are. It second-guesses reality. True science and true religion are non-ideological.

VI

True religion is the religion of the most truly kindly, gracious, anxiety- free, and unassuming persons. We've all known at least a few who are like that. It's their preparation for being that way. We usually just enjoy remembering such people. Is that enough?

Why should we not search out what makes them as they are?

Heightening is what goes on in true religion. To be heightened is to be, in effect, inwardly amended, made amenable to higher ways.

Heightening goes on in non-religious contexts when we lose ourselves in appreciation of the arts, act from compassion, or contemplate matters dispassionately even when they affect our fortunes. In true religion we taken heightening farther through beyonding.

Nota Bene: The understanding of height as superiority is built into our language—and into the universal human conceptual scheme. The higher is ideality, beneficence, nobility, wisdom, comprehension, competency. That we share height as quality appears integral to what we have, and may, become (a consideration which might or might not support a teleology).

Heightening is the highest common denominator of the major religions. To be heightened is ultimately to live freeness while attending to what one must do. How do we know this? We know it because people have done it.

Whatever practices, rituals, and beliefs true religion happens to incorporate support heightening and aren't substitutes for it. Apart from it, they're nothing.

When there's heightening, it's initially as though your will is agreeably dissolved. It releases you from your baser interests and predilections, shifting your attraction to higher ones. It's sometimes called spiritual growth and sublimation.

To those who'd denigrate heightening as an ideal, I reply: Revisit the worst thing you've done. Recollect the shame of it and how it darkened your existence. Would you consent to have effaced from your history that harm done and that self-reproach? If so, you can appreciate heightening. So I'd ask you: If being heightened is desirable that far, why not farther, then farther, then farther?

The scientific study of true religion is the scientific study of heightening: of what it's like, how it alters us, and all that it can be detected to result from and in.

Scientists can begin by interviewing those who've impressively undergone heightening. They can then undergo it themselves. They can do this with their wills and emotions engaged, while their intellects observe independently.

At first the scientific study of religion will have to be phenomenological: descriptive rather than analytical. Thereafter the effort will be to evolve the process toward replication of experiences, predictability, and mathematical precision. How far that can be done is presently unanswerable. That matters less than does recognizing the desirability of the undertaking.

In heightening, minds are brought up from the unsublimated sex drive, the impression of embodiment (sometimes with body-consciousness disappearing), and the anxiety over mortality. The more headway we make in true religion, the more the grip of those on us is loosened and the less afraid we are.

Scientists can undergo this. They can check into the mind and brain concomitants of it.

If we identify true religion with heightening, science has a standard by which to evaluate religion. Shouldn't the result be what counts in religion, as in science?

Religions teach strenuous mental and physical disciplines and wholehearted worship as among the means of initiating and enhancing heightening. Scientists can perform them with, so to speak, one eye open. By that I don't mean insincerely, but with inspecting the process as one objective of precipitating it, so as to know it from both within and without.

Once heightening has commenced, there may be lengthy periods when nothing seems to be taking place. The rule then is to carry on undismayed, as we don't always know what's going on in us. After a time of quiet, it's not uncommon for a great deal to happen at once. Scientists should be mindful of this pattern and be patient and persistent.

Well-known themes from religions, such as bowing down and repentance, constitute the subjugation of the lower tendencies of the persona, anticipatory to one's being heightened. They bring with them relief and exaltation. Scientists can weigh testimony and can themselves feel what comes of them.

The major religions give us tools to perform heightening with. People are heightened both in theistic religions such as Judaism, Islam, Zoroastrianism, and Christianity, and in non-theistic religions such as Buddhism, Jainism, Daoism, and the Advaita branch of Hinduism. None of these religions is untrue if heightening is the standard of religious truth.

Prayer is comprehended immediately by everyone. It's instinctual. It's our heartfelt blending with our more elevated possibilities. It becomes the receiving of high gifts such as unselfishness, lovingness, courage, and trust.

It has been argued that there can't be a heaven (or heavens, as we can conceive of many heavenly states or abodes) because space venturers and astronomers have seen nothing of the kind "up there." This misses the unvarying references to the heavenly as higher in the sense of being purer and subtler—that is, in the sense of heightening—than the material, and so as not visible to material eyes.

As we've had argonauts and astronauts, so one day, I predict, we'll have *rarenauts* to explore what can be known only through the rarefaction of the mental.

Some may feel that for scientists to undergo any enduring revision of their internal lives is too much to ask, that it'd be onerous. But it could be that it's what they'll leave behind that they'll thereafter recollect as onerous. And what science finds onerous is ignorance.

VII

The process of heightening can make us aware of the higher. It's to the higher that all religions direct us.

I call it the higher because that's the notion we get of its nature. I don't capitalize, because I intend the term as less a name than a characterization. "The higher" might refer to a compound entity or to a condition of entities; I'm content to have it remain indefinite.

The higher is unlike everything else that we know, which isn't to say that it's unlike everything else that is. Its being higher is the surest thing we gather about it. The higher is simply what's higher in the sense of better and is what heightening takes us to.

It's only sometimes that we think of the higher as God. It needn't manifest as a person or a dimension or a state of being or as the same twice. Belief in God is receptivity to the higher. But so is all religious practice.

How do we know that the higher is? Subjectively it seems that in one's being heightened what one encounters is beyond oneself, and that's by definition the higher, whatever the self's true boundaries may be.

The higher is better intuited than conceptualized, as we don't know how or even whether it's finite.

We may meet with a vision or a miracle or something else not routine, something indicative of the higher's reality or of the objective as answerable to the subjective. I'll refer you here to the remainder of this book, in especial to the chapters on faith, imagination, and the miraculous.

It may well be that there's no unmediated knowing of the higher except as, and commensurately with, one's being raised, refined, made free, through involvement with it.

A scientist who wants to investigate true religion will have to do it internally, then, because that's where it is. The aim should be to undergo heightening and engage the higher by whatever means turn out to be availing.

According to many religious persons, the higher responds to us as we respond to it. Can scientists enter into dialogue with the higher? Why not see? There might be a reply to interest that's conjoined with humility and a readiness to be of assistance to everyone's spiritual strivings. Highness of motivation could be the activating ingredient, if we go by anecdotal evidence.

Why shouldn't how we can most productively address ourselves to the higher be a question as much for science as for religion? But it can't be answered with our intellects alone. If we approach life only intellectually, we weaken our intuition, lessening our larger awareness.

No facility at reasoning suffices if our instincts are bad. Scientific investigators can cultivate their intuition and not suppress it, so as to notice the difference. What should be asked of them is not that they believe things about what's beyond us, even as to whether anything is "there," but that they go toward such a possibility with wondering and ready minds.

Unreceptiveness to the higher is intellectual narcissism at its worst and a senseless diminution of whatever transhuman prospects humanity may have. Why say it has none, when its having some would make of life so much more than most of us unthinkingly think it is?

The changes associated with true religion make for insecurity, which many escape into—depending on their predilections—hedonism, rationalism, or fundamentalism. The religious depersonalizes, as personhood is limitation. Yet the greatest love, in which the greatest security is experienced, is love that's universal and therefore impersonal, synonymous with the annihilation of oneself as a being with definite and permanent borders. This makes religiousness reliant on intuitiveness.

Intuitiveness is direct knowing. It shades into wisdom. They aren't identical insofar as the wise are always intuitive while others are intuitive only now and then.

In intuitiveness/wisdom, one is already present with information, as distinguished from one's having to arrive at it. The accuracy of this assertion can be scientifically examined.

This same presumed non-separation of knower and known may be what's visible in "idiot savants" who can provide accurate mathematical answers instantly, effortlessly, and, so far, inexplicably. It's thought that ultra-rapid brain calculations make this occur; but another possibility is that there's no anterior event, simply immediate detection of the answer.

Again, a miracle appears to occur without causality: that is, minus all of the intervening steps that we've been taught to presume necessary. Paranormal events are of this kind, as when lights that have no wiring or bulbs reportedly go on in haunted houses. Wouldn't it be useful to find out conclusively the truth of such claims?

If you could trace an instance of causality far enough, you might find that it connects to all that is ("the butterfly effect"). It's as though everything causes everything, with degrees of directness. But within the miraculous, the impression is that everything causes nothing and that there's some different avocatory dynamic at work.

We can't yet judge whether a miracle has to be performed by an agent with "supernatural" abilities, or whether it can take place spontaneously and devoid of agency (perhaps in answer to an inherent ripeness in a situation or a person).

To say that there are no miracles is to deny justice to an enormous quantity of testimony, some of it present-day and well investigated. We may not know *what* miracles are, but to refuse to consider *whether* they are requires more "faith" than would a humble "maybe."

Closely allied to intuition, miracles, and paranormality is mysticism.

Mysticism is the most heightening heightening. To some mystics, the higher is attainable as dazzlingly beyond what our intellects can grasp, the apogee of what we can know/be. Scientists could endeavor to undergo that.

The yogis of ancient India discerned within themselves what may be the native patterns and metamorphoses of being. Their unparalleled disclosures are immortalized in the Vedas. The Buddha mapped for us a route to transformative insight. Alchemists sought formulae for transmuting the psyche's "lead" into "gold." Meister Eckhardt, Teresa of Avila, Jakob Boehme, Sri Aurobindo, and others made some of their higher experiences public. Perhaps several million less-known figures have done similar things by internal observation and experimentation.

Why is so little that's comparable being attempted by scientists today? And why should those who wish to do so start by manipulating the brain, when that isn't how it has been done?

What mystics undergo is not only vastly more enjoyable but vastly more conducive to intelligent living than are getting drunk or getting drugged or getting sexual or getting entertained, our everyday answers to the stresses and frustrations of our conventional "reality."

VIII

The humans who've taken religion farthest I'll dub allors, because they naturally identify with all—with all human beings, all beings, and all of being. Quite a few such persons—those I described above as "the more than good"—are known to history and to ourselves.

Allors are traditionally designated in different places by such terms as sage, jnani, saint, wali, jivanmukta, sadguru, Zen master, qutub, avatar, salik, and pir. Religions, even civilizations, are traceable to one or more allors: think of Zoroaster, Muhammad, Moses, the Buddha, Lao Tzu, Jesus, the rishis of ancient India, the ten Sikh gurus.

Singly, they're enormously important to us; all together, oddly, they count for nothing in our estimation. Now that overviews of religion are common, that circumstance can be reconsidered.

Allors haven't come into conflict or disagreed broadly with one another, however dissimilar their depictions of how things are may appear at a glance to have been. According to what some of them have said, their differences are strategic only. None has declared otherwise.

Allors inhabit our own time, and not only olden times. The chapter on higher humanity describes some current and recent ones and discusses how true ones can be told.

Scientists can hope to observe, interview, and engage allors and work out what they're like. They can take instruction from them in varieties of meditation and whatever else is proffered them. They can do this both for themselves and for humanity, with generous intentions and without self-importance.

It's unreasonable for fundamentalists to condemn followers of another religion for following an allor, which is what they themselves profess to do. It's unreasonable for rationalists to forget allors when trying to weigh religions which wouldn't have existed without them.

We get a sense of wisdom, which is our highest approach to knowledge, from allors and those influenced by them; we learn to reproduce it somewhat within ourselves through familiarity with, and concentration on, what they've said.

Allors are the kindlers of the divine in the human. Most Western religion is cooling ashes, not because it's Christian but because it has parted company with wisdom so as to ally itself with tradition, literalness toward scriptures, consensus, faction, and the opinions of official theologians and church leaders.

Allors have said they aren't omniscient but can know whatever the situation requires them to know, and that their knowing of the outer world occurs inside themselves. If investigation affords reason to credit that, we can theorize about what I'll call *the introverse,* a fused subjectivity and objectivity which, in some regards, it may be possible for humanity to draw upon for knowledge of how things stand and what to do concerning them.

To restore wisdom to religion and the world would be first of all to give ear to contemporary allors.

Social repression taking its cues from someone's scriptures is a problem that could give way if it were our custom to appeal to allors. Luther said it's "not for Herr Everybody" to interpret the Bible. Today, however, the Bible and the Qur'an are altogether at the mercy of Herr Everybody's often small understanding. Let it be the wise and not the foolish to whom we listen about our sacred writings.

According to themselves, what allors are is what humanity will be. So you'd suppose that living allors would attract the curiosity of students of evolution and be sought out by the religious. Yet as a rule neither religion nor science pays them notice.

Allorance is a word I make you a present of, to designate how allors live and are. (It's pronounced AWL-or-ance.) Being allorant means caring about everyone and not giving preference to oneself or one's own kind. Jesus' parable of the Good Samaritan is a tale illustrative of allorance.

We've long termed the ideal social attitude "acceptance" and "tolerance." But the language of that is encumbered with unintended implications. Who wants to be tolerated, like a nuisance? Who wants to be accepted, like a tragically inescapable fate? It's otherwise with allorance. The allorant are always with and for all who are. Scientists could seek out the preconditions and the accompaniments of that achievement.

(If some fear that to be with all is to be with the worst of the worst, my rejoinder is that it's to be with the best of the best and what they know and can do when faced with the worst of the worst.)

Allorance is about love and universality, which naturally go together, as we can't love anyone in the completest sense till we can love everyone in the completest sense. It excludes none, though this doesn't imply being passive in the face of evildoing or being continually and explicitly in dialogue with everyone. It's less entire withness than entire readiness for a summons to any withness at all.

People who relate themselves to allors and imbibe their influence I'll call allorists. High allorists are those most actuated not by a religion but by contact with an allor.

When we can enthusiastically perform difficult service even for those who hate and harm us, nothing so exalts our mood and contributes to our peacefulness. And rationalists should recognize that that's conducive to thinking rationally, since it drives away fright and partiality.

Rationalists may say that they approve of loving one's neighbor and having peace of mind but can do these things without religion. Ah, but it isn't so easy! The allor Baba Lokenath said we can "transcend even death" if we're able to remain unaffected by three kinds of assault on ourselves: "abusive and insulting words", "separation from loved ones", and "losing wealth". (In Danger Remember Me, Kolkata, Lokenath Divine Life Mission, 1991, p.141) People allergic to spirituality have no way of remaining indifferent to such blows.

IX

Infallibility is often imputed to the recorded words of previous allors. There's nothing infallible, however, about those who read those words today.

Fundamentalists and rationalists take religious beliefs—about what befell the ancients, what comprises human nature, what heavenly beings are like, what they want from us, what will happen on earth one day, etc.—to necessarily be assertions of purported fact. It's that assumption about them that again and again breeds trouble while doing no one any good.

Mightn't true religion be true in the sense that the sound of a bell is true—that of representing the best of what it exemplifies—and not in the sense that a proposition is true—that of directing us to something separate as the confirmation of its veracity?

If you look over the chief religions, you'll see that facts don't interest them. When the Bible says to honor your father and your mother, for example, it doesn't say to do so only if they deserve it. It isn't about what kinds of persons they are, but about what kind of person you'll be.

And loving our neighbors may not be made easier by attending to the facts about them. In true religion we don't study past or present facts but experience what makes for higher future ones.

I concluded in <u>Against</u> <u>Fundamentalism</u> that a religion's stories, doctrines, and over-all depictions are most helpfully defined not as factual claims but as means of bringing about devotion. Hindu myths are the clearest case in point. A religious myth makes the higher accessible to us by, so to speak, letting us breathe its pure air.

I'm not saying that just any beliefs will do religiously. Whether that's true remains to be determined. I'm saying that the combination of long-prescribed beliefs and an earnest desire to be heightened and of service can make all the difference.

What good can beliefs do us if they're factually accurate but we don't address them devotionally? A fact is merely a fact unless something is made of it with feeling and imagination. Scientists could test what goes into and comes out of that.

So I suggest that what religions appear to tell us about the world isn't information. It performs another function and should be viewed by science accordingly. I suggest, too, that the best people don't treat their religious beliefs as information. They don't use them to impute objective rightness to themselves and objective wrongness to others.

Religious beliefs I propose to define, then, as *loftlore*. I mean that they fashion a conjunction of us and the higher, aiding in our heightening. Were what religions tell us to be considered loftlore and not information, we might do much more right and much less wrong in acting for our religions.

I suspect that religious beliefs, taken the right way, very ingeniously open new passageways in our minds and brains, creating something rather than reflecting something.

(This isn't a position I've fallen back to because science has brought down some religious beliefs. It's my position of first choice and the one I'd expect people with free and intelligent minds to choose.)

I don't say that loftlore has to be only loftlore, that there *can't* be other dimensions to it. I say that the factual isn't its dimension—even if some of what it relates is factually correct.

What, then, does true religion amount to? I'll say it's the activity that seeks advanced individual heightening; that uses traditional beliefs and rituals and practices, when it does, for that and for nothing else; and that characteristically pays heed to at least one allor.

The votaries of a religion begin to sour when they care more about what people believe than about their undergoing heightening and having access to the wisdom of living allors. Then they objectify their scriptures, and ill will and woundings and conflagrations ensue.

Rationalists act as though true religion didn't exist and all religion were fundamentalistic. That begs the question. How can they favor reason but disfavor logic? How can they advocate science but despise evidence? In taking the true measure of religion, they'd have to consider the glorious and not the inglorious alone.

It's rational to look not to rationalists but to allors and true scientists for insights into religion. The key is for true religion to be distinguished everywhere from false. I've suggested how, the criterion being the sole emphasis of true religion on heightening and allorance and infinintention and on a religion's beliefs as loft-lore rather than as factuality. Then true religion can be the laboratory in which true science acquaints itself with the higher.

TWO

INVESTIGATING RELIGION

I

How are the religious and the paranormal related? We have no clear answer presently. Why don't we get one?

If we decide how to address the paranormal, that should help us decide how to investigate the religious. But there's no agreement on how to do that. So further along in this chapter I'm going to propose a convention that can do away with that discrepancy.

The religious and the paranormal overlap in the area of life after death, part of which has to do with haunting and ghostly apparitions, and in the area of the miraculous; it's the former of these and what we should make of it that I'll take up next.

Recently a student paranormal research group at a university near me held a large conference. Two professors in scientific subjects were mentioned in the campus newspaper as deploring that and opposing university funding for the student group. I e-mailed to both of them. I truthfully didn't know how they'd justify their position, and I hoped they'd make that clear to me.

I include what these professors said because they're representative—I think fairly so—of rationalistic scientists.

I inquired of one professor, "Perhaps you'd tell me in the briefest terms what you would recommend as a scientific way of investigating paranormal claims? I'm curious to know." He replied immediately with words that seemed friendly. He recommended I read Carl Sagan's <u>The Demon Haunted World</u> (New York, Ballantine Books, 1996), which I promptly did.

He also said, "Real scientists make measurements using instruments that are known to measure what they are purported to measure and they employ those instruments in responsible ways. Pseudoscientists do things like listening to white noise for hours trying to find bits that sound like voices of ghosts, or interpreting changes in electromagnetic fields as they walk around a house as the presence of ghosts when such fields are known to vary normally due to the presence of electrical appliances, powerlines, etc." Yes, but you don't know what instruments can measure, besides what they were designed for, unless you experiment; and how clearly you make out the "ghost voices" from the background noise on the tape is pertinent to whether or not they're indicative of an anomaly.

If what affects the researchers' electrical equipment at a given time in a reputedly haunted house isn't picked up at other times, and if it's observed to change location within the house so that regular influences like power lines and electrical appliances don't account for it, then there's evidence of something apart from the usual, though what that is isn't thereby brought out.

A decided electrical spike might correlate with something seen or felt or heard, such as an apparition, or a cold spot, or an orb subsequently found on a videotape of the scene from that moment, or a possible voice that a tape recorder picked up just then. Correlations among such factors provide reason to think something is "up."

If you got an electrical reaction that was strong and unexplained *and* that moved to another spot *and* that was accompanied by a sudden drop in the mercury of a thermometer *and* by the sighting of something out of the corner of your eye *and* by the appearance of something unexplained on the tape *and* by intelligible voice-like sounds on the tape recorder, I don't think even a rationalist could say that nothing was going on there, or that what was going on was all in someone's head. This wouldn't mean that there are ghosts, just that questions and further investigation are appropriate. I think that's beyond argument.

The professor also wrote, "Real science involves designing experiments that test the assumptions of the experimenter. Pseudoscience often involves the opposite—anecdotes ('I heard a noise!' or 'It felt cold all of a sudden'), biased experiments ('ghost hunters' who don't find any ghosts probably have a hard time landing TV contracts), and willfully ignoring contradictory evidence when it's found." By the last of these I expect he meant evidence for natural explanations.

There's nothing wrong with anecdotes. Any detective will welcome them. They aren't proof, but they give you a starting place and a preliminary idea as to what you're dealing with. And if paranormal investigators, or some of them, have an incentive to cheat, so do those who set out to disprove the existence of the paranormal; actions by persons on *both* sides have in fact met with controversy over the years, attended by bitter exchanges of accusations.

He further wrote: "Real scientific disciplines show progress. For any real scientific discipline (like biology) you'll find that there are things we know about it now that we didn't know 10, 20, or 50 years ago. What progress has been made in our knowledge of demons or ESP?" I don't know about ESP or demons, but discoveries have been made that suggest a connection between hauntings and such factors as ambient energy, nearby water, and—in cases of multiple and pronounced phenomena—ley lines. With the improvement of electrical equipment, it's possible much more will be learned. At least, I wouldn't bet it won't be.

However, even if we had no glimmer beyond what was known centuries ago about hauntings, should that cause us to say they're unreal? Their nature might just be such that nothing more can be learned about them through existing means. That would call for coming up with additional means, not quitting.

He added: "Real scientists know that one study doesn't mean

anything. They repeat each others' experiments until a body of evidence is developed and then they examine it dispassionately to evaluate the originally-posed hypothesis. Pseudoscientists, on the other hand, are only interested in confirming their apriori beliefs. A mountain of evidence showing no reason to believe in ESP or dowsing [he referred, I think, to the failure of experiments to confirm expectations about them] means very little to the pseudoscientist, who rationalizes that the phenomenon doesn't work when non-believers are present, etc." Certainly duplication of results must be sought. And investigators can be asked to put aside any excess of disbelief, as they should have no such attitude in any case.

Is it true that all or most paranormalists "are only interested in confirming their apriori beliefs"? Isn't that opinion itself an apriori belief? Is it based on a scientific sampling? Such a sweeping *ad hominem* characterization doesn't strike me as cricket. The few paranormalists I've met, for what it's worth, have been anxious to find out what's going on, just as scientists are. It's possible they intended to cheat, or would at times, but I'm not prepared to assume so.

If you've an alert mind, you've noticed that in what I quoted the professor didn't answer my question, which was "(W)hat (would) you...recommend as a scientific way of investigating paranormal claims?" Neither did he answer it in the brief, unquoted parts of his e-mail. He said that parapsychology is "pseudoscience" but didn't say how "real science" would address something like a haunting.

I asked the second professor, "Perhaps you could tell me very briefly what you would recommend as a scientifically acceptable approach to the study of paranormal phenomena? I'm curious as to what you had in mind." He replied with four possible interpretations of my question, none of which I intended or was necessarily implied by it.

In response I said, "Say someone sees a ghost, for example. How would you look into that situation with an eye to determining what the phenomenon was and what produced it?" He said,

"For more than a century there have been many determined attempts to investigate 'ghosts, spirit manifestations, demon possession,' etc. Whenever accepted scientific safeguards against fraud or self-delusion are followed, the results are nil."

To say that the results are nil is to say, surely, that there's no proof. But now the issue becomes what constitutes scientific proof as opposed to anecdotal evidence. For anecdotal evidence of haunted buildings and ghosts abounds.

Most people may be unaware of it, but scientific proof is pretty narrow. For example, if four investigators in the same room and at the same moment saw an apparition, heard a seeming voice, agreed later on what they had understood it to say, and felt themselves to be touched by something just then, that'd seem to most of us to be rather persuasive proof that something besides themselves was there. But from the standpoint of scientific investigation it'd be merely anecdotal.

To prove the existence of the entity so perceived, the investigators would have to specify conditions that'd reliably precede its manifestations. Ideally, they'd be able to cause it to appear at will.

Given that a ghost is invariably said to be somewhat like a living human, and insofar as it isn't under the control of its investigators, there's no immediately evident way of scientifically proving its existence, though anyone who underwent the experiences I alluded to, even scientists, would be likely to concede that it existed.

For science, then, only predictability yields proof. But for our everyday purposes, close exposure to a ghost under normal conditions would be thought to prove its reality. So there's a disconnection between how we live and scientific method.

That makes it easy for those hostile to the idea of the paranormal to dismiss it as unproven and therefore as delusion or folklore or fraud.

Why do rationalists reject the paranormal? I see two reasons. One is that it's redolent of the religious and so could give a religion leverage against science. The other is that there's a keen competition for funding within the scientific community, so that to admit a paranormalist of any stature whatever into the "club" would be to potentially reduce the money available to one's preferred colleagues and to dilute their prestige and the attention they can command.

As I just said, there's a gap between scientific method and our daily lives. Not even the most scrupulous scientist will decline to cross a street because it hasn't been scientifically proved that no traffic is approaching at a near distance. And that can be a matter of life and death!

Nor, typically, have the most exacting scientists chosen their spouses scientifically or even primarily on the basis of objective considerations. It'd be tough for them to argue that there's no room in life for anything but scientific decision-making when they themselves demonstrate the contrary each day.

The professor further wrote, "(T)he public postings of (the student group) worry me greatly because of their potential to be dangerously misleading in terms of both what they purport to accomplish and the supposed authority for their activities. Just this past weekend I read of a pair of parents in the US who burned their baby in a microwave oven because they believed that it was possessed by Satan (the baby, not the over). I consider such thoughts manifestly delusional, and believe...people who purport to take them seriously as phenomena to be investigated as potentially valid...to be contemptibly irresponsible." But the paranormal group had done nothing resembling that.

There's a difference between listening tentatively to someone said to have *experienced* a haunting and uncritically listening to someone who holds bizarre *beliefs*.

Not atypically, persons who report encountering a ghost don't, or formerly didn't, "believe in ghosts." And there's no reason why such a person couldn't remain open to an indefinite number of possible interpretations of what that experience comes down to or implies.

One thing is certain: if those parents had been detached and curious, as true scientists are, and had been prepared to discuss what was going on and decide what to do only in consultation with representatives of the wider community, the baby would still be alive. Without closed minds there could've been no such tragedy. Hasn't the professor himself displayed a closed mind toward the paranormal? And, on the other hand, is there anything to being a paranormalist that necessitates having a closed mind?

But again, the professor's limits and biases are not only his but those of rationalism, and that's what I want to bring out here.

The reports of hauntings are many and from everywhere. You hear them, sometimes first-hand, from people you know. You read them in newspapers and books. The literature on them is voluminous. Persons with steady lives and good mental health aren't immune to the "ghostly." In even my rather small circle of acquaintances are at least three who've seen ghosts, and they seem to be no different from my other acquaintances.

The professor added, "If I had an acquaintance who, as you wrote, 'sees a ghost, for example,' I would suggest that they begin with simple lifestyle modifications such as getting more sleep and/or using less in the way of psychotropic chemicals (alcohol, caffeine, etc.). If the impressions continued, I would suggest consultation with some responsible person with genuine professional medical training." If he wanted to argue that whoever sees a ghost *must* be mentally aberrant, either at that moment or in general, then he was obligated to—and didn't—propose that that notion be tested scientifically.

Instead he treated the absence of scientific proof of ghosts as bestowing on us a *fact* (the nonexistence of ghosts) from which an *inference* (that whoever sees one is mentally ill) can be derived. That's reasoning that I'm confident no reasonable person can regard as reasonable.

Competent psychologists or psychiatrists wouldn't declare a person mentally impaired solely on the basis of that person having seen a ghost; they'd evaluate the entire personality. If the sighting occurred in a place where others had reported having comparable experiences, that'd be all the more reason to be wary of letting a single factor decide the matter.

Since the professor had offered me a case of people (the baby-killing couple) who were deluded, I offered him one of people who aren't. I quoted to him, and I quote to you in Chapter Six of this book, e-mails that I received from a woman I've known for many years who is sane and truthful and not desirous of notoriety. She's a university graduate in early middle age who lives a productive life, isn't a drinker or a drugger, and is a person of firm character who knows how to think critically, recognize further possibilities, and test propositions.

The "presences" in her house were detected by two humans and reacted to by two dogs. So there were multiple witnesses of multiple species; and multiple senses (sight, hearing, and touch) were involved. Again, I'm not saying we know anything conclusive about what went on there, just that trying to find out more about that situation and ones like it is warranted.

And what did the professor have to say about that? "I can think of no better illustration (than your several, increasingly lengthy communications) of the importance that the...University take all possible steps to dissociate itself clearly and definitely from its apparent fascination with paranormal phenomena." He also stated that he would reply to no further correspondence from me.

If he felt that I was taking up his time unproductively, as he implied, he might've shortened things by simply answering what I asked him in the first place. But perhaps he believes it must never be conceded that the paranormal exists, or science will give way and we'll be overrun by by superstition and madness?

He and his colleague may think that they did answer my question, after a fashion, by referring me to a website. The second professor had written in his first e-mail: "Those who are interested in 'paranormal research' (as I am not) have a most attractive course of action open to them. They can go to the web site of the James Randi Educational Foundation (www.randi.org/research/challenge/htm) and make application to document paranormal findings objectively, according to mutually-agreed protocols, with the prospect of winning one million dollars for any successful documentation." In fact this challenge is nowadays open only to celebrities, not that I found it "attractive" anyway.

James "The Amazing" Randi is a professional magician who has for years investigated claims of the paranormal with the intention of discrediting them. He has since 1964 offered money to whoever can prove that the paranormal exists. However, as I noted above, such claims are by their very nature hard to prove scientifically. That's particularly true in the case of a haunting. Anything at all uncertain or requiring interpretation can be disallowed as subjective. And not everyone who has lived through such events is tempted by the money or wishes to be made a public spectacle.

I didn't notice at first that the professor, beginning with his initial reply, was carbon-copying our correspondence to several persons, including the anti-paranormalist Randi and the outspoken rationalist Richard Dawkins (for the latter of whom see the next chapter). As I had thought it was a personal correspondence, and as I'm not well-known, this struck me as strange. But contemporary rationalism is fast going from tendency to movement, and he apparently took me to be challenging that movement's tenets and potentially threatening public acceptance of it.

II

How would I go about researching something like a haunting? I'd use common sense, as the best paranormalists do, and I'd emphasize interviews, observation, background research, and documentation. I'd especially be interested in how the various phenomena—visual, auditory, electronic, etc.—fit together. If scientific proof isn't possible, what *is* possible is the development of a preliminary verdict of relative likelihood.

Where ghosts are concerned, I don't want to hear "Not proved, ever—end of story." I want an acknowledgement that humanly significant circumstances are present. Scientists as such may not care about that, but most of us do as human beings.

I'll designate humanly significant circumstances "HS." The concept obtains when scientific proof is unavailable not because there's no evidence but because predictability and duplication of the precise phenomenon are ruled out by our inability to control the entity. To call the entity's existence a matter of human significance is to say that what may be discovered about it can legitimately make a difference to how we live and how we think. The world is one kind of place if we don't survive our deaths, for example, and another kind if we do.

Within HS, I'd like the judgment potentially made to cite a new category: "strong anecdotal evidence," or SAE.

Weak anecdotal evidence might be a singular claim made without corroboration by a person of unknown truthfulness. In a case such as the one I described above, the evidence is fairly strong. Again, the aim isn't to parlay that into proof, but to determine what's a good candidate for further investigation.

To those who say that the goal of science is proof, I say that progressive discovery can be another. To those who say that what I'm proposing would drive a wedge among scientists, I say, It's about time, lest the best of them be at the mercy of the ideologues.

Scientific method evolved by fitting its practices to the circumstances. If rationalistic scientists are going to adhere to a system of investigation that wasn't designed for and can't accommodate ghostly phenomena, then we the public have a right to recognize such a secondary category as "humanly significant" and such a determination within it as "strong anecdotal evidence." If those scientists won't join us in doing so, it's our right to question their objectivity and their rationality with regard to the paranormal.

Carl Sagan wrote in the book cited above: "(E)ven laws of Nature are not absolutely certain. There may be new circumstances never before examined—inside black holes, say, or within the electron, or close to the speed of light—where even our vaunted laws of Nature break down and, however valid they may be in ordinary circumstances, need correction." (p.28) I could suggest that a haunting is such a circumstance, though not a new one. However, I won't ask that the laws be changed, just that conditions to which they don't recommend themselves be recognized as such and that the investigation of those conditions not be compared to our automatically conferring credibility on the opinions of persons who bake babies in ovens.

At present we have scientists dismissing hauntings and the like on the ground that there's no scientific proof of them, while enthusiastic amateurs are announcing that what they've come up with is that proof. There has to be a third alternative. I ask that trained scientists, who recognize that it's unrealistic to expect scientific proof of such occurrences, investigate them so as to assure (a) impartiality, and (b) the most accurate anecdotal evidence available. What we're in quest of is human significance and strong anecdotal evidence: HS/SAE. We aren't asking that that be called proof, only that further steps be predicated on it.

As for the scarcity of funding for such work, I'm confident that private, no-strings-attached contributions to a foundation set up for the purpose can raise more than sufficient money to make this happen if reputable scientists are onboard with it. Interest in such things runs wide and deep, as I don't think even a rationalist could dispute.

It's pertinent that a culture war is going on in our time with rationalists on one side and everyone else on the other. That, too, has human consequences. I'd rather not live in a world where a family undergoes harrowing things in its home but is unable to discuss them or ask for help because of intimidation by persons who want the paranormal denied rather than examined. For my taste that's too much like the incarceration of political dissidents in mental hospitals in the late Union of Soviet Socialist Republics.

One advantage of HS/SAE is that because it doesn't involve scientific proof, each of us is free to decide individually what we think about it. When something *is* proved, there's a demand that everyone agree about it. That has social and political ramifications, which I'll discuss in the next chapter.

Sciists, as I term non-religious but also non-rationalist scientists, have a chance to contain what they dislike in rationalist

thinking by overseeing investigations into the paranormal themselves and/or lending their prestige as scientists to the proposition that it deserves and can reward study.

III

Science doesn't require proof if it's to tell us something—
about the paranormal or about the religious. In its theories and
its determinations, all it requires is gradations of promisingness.
What seems least promising—say, a claim that the world was
created by Martians who are gradually devouring it—can be as-
signed a very low investigative priority in the absence of anything
indicative of its being the case. The more and the better the evidence for the truth of a thesis, the more promising it can be said
to be.

Whether a theory fits with existing theories should be im-
material to its promisingness. Scientists' dedication should be to
carefulness and thoroughness, never to the conservatism that'd
turn away surprising data or stifle second thoughts.

I've said that religious beliefs can be considered loftlore,
which means they don't require proof or even evidence of factuality because they aren't all-purpose claims. What justifies them
is their devotional usage. So it isn't beliefs I want to go into here.
Rather, it's experiences.

Here's one example. I find that if I address myself to the
elephant-headed Hindu deity Ganesh (also called Ganesha and
Ganapati and Vinayakar), I feel more connection than I feel
when addressing other deities. Now, of course that's subjective
and only one person's impression. But do any research and you
may read that other worshipers have experienced the same thing,
to the extent that there's a consensus about it. That's a place to
start from. It entails HS (human significance), with some degree
of anecdotal evidence. Where should we go from there?

I'd have people make themselves available to Ganesh, patiently and sincerely, in the manner of worship, and in a noticing
mode.

I'd have this done by non-Hindus, as that lessens previous

conditioning. The experimenters must put aside their beliefs about the situation and just want to observe what develops. Let's see who experiences this connectedness or feeling of devotion to Ganesh, who experiences it toward other deities instead, and who experiences it toward all or toward none of them.

If it turns out that the sense of connection is felt more with Ganesh, or with any deity, than with the others, then it's a matter of finding out why that is. One thing to do is to see what else the persons in those different categories have in common with one another that they don't have in common with those in the other categories. Now we're moving from a subjectivity that's individual to a subjectivity that's shared.

Experiments will be in order. As Ganesh has the head of an animal, responsiveness to the jackal-headed Egyptian deity Anubis can be checked, as can responsiveness to animal or partly animal gods and goddesses from any tradition. Deities can be invented and appealed to. Where to take the research next can be decided at each step. The idea is that we may understand slightly more about worship and what it evokes as we go along.

If it should be found that Ganesh is inexplicably discerned to be more approachable than are other deities, then we've discovered one factor that may have application somewhere along the line as we proceed. We can compare him with Jesus in this regard, for one thing. And we can compare worshipers of Ganesh—and/or of another Hindu deity who stands out in some respect—with Christians, with Jews, with Muslims, with Buddhists, etc., to see wherein they're alike and different.

The idea isn't to find out which religion is best, as there are excellent people and terrible people in all of them. It's to see what's what—and what might be most helpful to members of the religions as they strive to be positive and humane. (As rationalists view religions as exerting mainly baleful influences, one would suppose they'd want to discover what in religion could offset those influences.)

In the previous chapter I referred to our examining of the process of heightening. Let's see what we can find out from it in connection with aesthetics, altruism, and worship. Again, we're looking for correlations, correlations, and more correlations.

I also mentioned our making application to the higher, as such. That can be done in various ways and the results described. When the same results are obtained by several persons, what those persons have in common can be determined.

The miraculous can be researched. Those who say they've experienced it can be interviewed and their credibility considered, and the circumstances of their alleged undergoings can be documented. Likelihood can be assessed. More can be learned about the miraculous in one fashion or another. If that's vague, ways of preciding it for the objective at hand can be worked out.

Mystics can be sought out and studied. Researchers can undertake mysticism and can see what it correlates with and what facilitates it and what impedes it.

In all of this the movement should be to intersubjectivity, objectivity, predictability, and statistical confirmation.

There has to be, before anything else, a will to do these things. For too long we've been in conflict with ourselves over the "faith" demanded of us within religions and the rationalist "faith" which says that all such factors have to be bogus. It's time to be empirical, open-minded, imaginative, and truly willing to know more.

How anyone could oppose that is difficult to conceive. Yet people will—and vehemently. But persons of intelligence and good will won't be deterred.

THREE

THE BARBARISM OF THE RATIONALIST MIND

I

Four recent books are the prongs of the new rationalism's jabbing pitchfork. The four are The God Delusion (2006) by Richard Dawkins, a prominent evolutionary biologist; Breaking the Spell (2006) by Daniel C. Dennett, an academic philosopher with a biological focus; The End of Faith (2004) by Sam Harris, a neurobiologist; and god is Not Great: How Religion Poisons Everything (2007) by Christopher Hitchens, a well-known journalist and critic.

You could be tempted to diffidence by these writers' imposing professional credentials. But those should make us demand all the more that they live up to the highest intellectual standards. Instead, they've all written as though true religion were unheard of.

It has been a century since Swami Ram Tirth said that you can understand a man only by loving him. These writers apparently believe that you can understand a religion only by hating it. As you may have guessed, my view is that you can understand a religion only through understanding *religion*, and that you can't understand *religion* without an implicit understanding of beyonding, infinintention, heightening, allorance, and loftlore; if your intellect doesn't provide that, your instincts nevertheless should if they're doing their job.

These books are compromised from the beginning by preju-

dice. Any scientific-minded and rational review of religion pre-
supposes neutrality toward it, but these writers are anything but
impartial or undecided. They all declare themselves atheists and
commend unbelief.

And if only defective religion—uninformed, deluded, big-
oted—counts as religion, why doesn't only defective science—
bungling, misinterpreting, cheating—count as science? How can
we compare the best of one field with the worst of another and
conclude anything meaningful?

These four entertain a conviction—an ominous one—that
people whose ideas are unlike their own are irrational on that account. The test of one's rationality isn't the ideas one starts with
but whether one is prepared to discuss them courteously, think
about them analytically when there's occasion to, and then modify them to conform to evidence and reason. Given their attitude, I'd ask if they themselves are prepared to do those things?

They think religion must be rationally indefensible if it came
into being through blind chance and not through divine intervention. However it came into being, it's rationally indefensible
only if heightening is rationally indefensible, as heightening is its
essence.

They indignantly cite endless instances of religious people
behaving inhumanly. But when something is as motivating as a
religion is, why *wouldn't* it be appropriated and abused by the
malevolent, the greedy, and the fanatically inclined?

They warn that religion could make this planet uninhabitable.
Reactiveness against the religious won't avert such an outcome.
Nor will the present concoction of ethics-blind technology, mo-
rality-blind science, and wisdom-blind culture, to which they offer no alternative.

They complain that scriptural verses make persecution and
warfare inevitable. What people make of a scripture says more
about them than about it. Like fundamentalists, rationalists
would deny the role of *interpretation*. In that, they're being deliberately unintelligent. The examples set by those who are wise
and benign are of more relevance than scriptural quotations are

to an apprehending of religion, as it's necessarily through one's level of character and insight that one interprets and applies a text.

If wisdom and not only information is what makes for the richest living, then contemporary science hasn't cornered the knowledge market. If superior comprehension and judgment are developed through spiritual life, then it's allors and not the Dawkinses, Harrises, Hitchenses, and Dennetts who are the trustworthy pathfinders. *Why not find out?*

It's rather well attested than shamans have demonstrated that they know things—about diseases and cures, conspicuously—in ways the rest of us don't. Scientists could do much more with that and with what shamans, mediums, and psychics believe, rightly or not, is their collaboration with spirits in obtaining information that's subsequently verified. *Why not find out?*

Dawkins: "(M)iracles, by definition, violate the principles of science." (p.59) And, in a debate with Christian geneticist Francis Collins in *Time* for November 13 2006, p.52: "Any belief in miracles is flatly contradictory not just to the facts of science but to the spirit of science." Whatever Dawkins may aver, there's no fact or spirit or principle belonging to science that's opposed to our uncovering whether or what the miraculous is. *Why not find out?*

He's saying theory (*I.e.* that there can't be miracles) should override evidence. That's not only unscientific but as anti-scientific as anything can be.

Dawkins' remark may be a fatal distortion of the requirement that scientists always try for a "natural" explanation. He confuses the *method* of science, which is naturalism, with the unscientific proposition that only the "natural" exists. As he has to know better, I can only figure he's trying to ensnare the ignorant as part of winning over public opinion.

What are your chances of coming across anything radically unlike what you're accustomed to if you avert your eyes? Rationalists don't like surprises. They don't like to admit ignorance. They have to be in control of whatever they address themselves to. But if anything about life is sure it's that sooner or later it'll deny us control, reveal our ignorance, and surprise us.

Those who best practice true religion delight in being surprised, in being disabused of mistaken ideas, and in implicitly yielding to what they conceive to be higher than themselves. It's they who adapt best, because they're alive to life and not disabled by anxieties or stuck with ideas they can't modify for fear of losing face or being shunned by their colleagues. Rationalism is a road that goes only to conformism.

Rationalists want existence to be a simple matter, with no higher reaches or profound mysteries. I *very* much suspect that it isn't in the least a simple matter. I suspect, in fact, that its variety and complexity and sheer amazingness extend to infinity. And I more than suspect that the human race—fighting against rationalists all the way, if need be—won't stop asking questions about it.

II

Lately rationalists have begun thinking bigger, alas. They're making plans for us.

Harris and Dawkins have designs on the traditional protections that religions enjoy in democratic societies, protections which also safeguard everyone else's thought and expression. They explicitly go after the democratically indispensable ideals of *tolerance* and *respect*, which they represent as bodyguards of dangerous irrationality.

I don't hear the other writers or those of like mind calling them to account for that. I take their silence to be tacit agreement. Alarms should be going off in our heads over this.

This is Harris against tolerance: "I hope to show that the very ideal of religious tolerance—born of the notion that every human being should be free to believe whatever he wants about God—is one of the principal forces driving us toward the abyss." (p.15) To him, divergence of opinion is an unaffordable luxury. To most of us, it's what polices and keeps open the road to truth.

Where disagreement isn't permitted, truth accommodates politics, rather than the reverse.

Dawkins against respect: "As long as we accept the principle that religious faith must be respected simply because it is religious faith, it is hard to withhold respect from the faith of Osama bin Laden and his suicide bombers." (p.306) Respecting "faith" is no different from respecting other opinion. To respect Bin Laden's opinion is to let him reach his own conclusions (not to let him blow us up) and to consider what he says. Disrespecting the opinions of those who differ with us comes down to disrespecting those who hold them and declining to hear them out. That comes down to denying that they could be even somewhat right. That comes down to treating one's own views as incontestable. That comes down to regarding oneself as infallible. Do we want our society run by people who think like that? Haven't we had enough of leaders who can't be told anything?

Harris against respect: "When was the last time that someone was criticzed for not 'respecting' another person's unfounded beliefs about physics or history? The same rules should apply to ethical, spiritual and religious beliefs as well." (p.176) They can't, so the analogy is false. In history and physics we call attention to people's mistakes and correct them using agreed-upon criteria. There are presently no such generally accepted criteria for spiritual, religious, or ethical positions. But that doesn't mean there's anarchy. The informed and sensible have disproportionate influence in society because the people tend to listen to them. Harris is overgeneralizing, making it seem that to permit the people to decide issues for themselves is to guarantee the triumph of ignorance over knowledge. The historical reality is that personal freedom and democracy have flourished alongside the sciences. We don't have to choose between science and democracy. No true friend of either would force such a choice on us.

Harris against tolerance: "(C)riticizing a person's faith is currently taboo in every corner of our culture. On this subject, liberals and conservatives have reached a rare consensus...But technology has a way of creating fresh moral imperatives. Our technical advances in the art of war have finally rendered our religious differences—and hence our religious *beliefs*—antithetical to our survival." (pp.13-14, italics in original) How many of us agree that intolerance is now a "fresh moral imperative" rather than *prima facie* evidence of a tyrannical disposition? Is being able to believe what recommends itself to you as true really too much to ask? And if you love God and try to bring peace to the world, are you working for doom? These notions are reaching for a drastic social paradigm shift. It'd have the severest political implications, too, which these books don't go into.

I'd say our best tools in religious disputes are loftlore, heightening, and allorance, not an attempt to outlaw religions. And religious views shade into philosophical views. Start forbidding some and you'll have to forbid more and more, because metaphysical thoughts spring up everywhere like dandelions.

What can enable people to live together in peace? The trick isn't to get everyone, worldwide, to agree, which they assuredly won't. It's to promote intelligent and honorable compromise and ongoing discussion aimed at removing the practical liabilities that attend our abstract disagreements.

By despising what others think and refusing to deal with them in a respectful and reasonable way, Harris and Dawkins would eliminate every alternative to armed conflict. And they'd do that in the name of reason!

They'd have us believe that tolerance and respect bespeak relativism while science has absolute, proven answers. But in science no theory is ever safe from new thinking, no method is ever safe from informed revision, and no proof is ever safe from what's discovered hereafter. Corrigibility is the *sine qua non* of thinking that's scientific and rational. Finality and absoluteness are alien to science, both in practice and within the true scientist's disposition.

This is not meant to imply that Darwinian evolution may be overthrown as we learn more. True science and true religion don't argue with facts, no matter what those facts are. True religion and true science can coexist and cross-pollinate because both are empirical and not dogmatic.

Even when scientists have a good explanation, they're alert for a better one or for a more satisfactory formulation of the same one. To true scientists, humility is a scientific virtue. To rationalists, it's a vice and a cop-out.

Finality is the battle flag of despotism. You might suppose a believer in reason would want more than anything to pull it down. But these writers would tear it from the hands of fundamentalists only to fasten it atop a juggernaut of their own.

The conviction that we ought to make up our own minds is as foundational as anything is to Western civilization. And right along we've anticipated that truth has what it takes to win out as long as all of us can speak up for what we find convincing. But Dawkins and Harris won't accord us the right to disagree with them. Dennett is more elusive, but he confers his approval on the other two; in keeping with what he writes, quoted below, about the complicity of sectarians who fail to denounce their followers who go too far, it may be that he shouldn't be absolved of responsibility for what they do. As for the volatile Hitchens, who began as a Trotskyist and now calls himself a Jeffersonian, his tilt toward rationalism makes it less than conclusive that we can count on him to preserve the deference to individualism and to perpetually open inquiry in every department of life that Jefferson bequeathed to us.

III

When people of some shared outlook convince themselves that they're of necessity solely and wholly in the right, as these writers have done, they cease being respectful, then tolerant, then amenable to democracy. There's no stopping after scuttling the first two, because the third depends on them. Do you see that? Do they?

Their self-assigned unique rightness, moreover, is fostered by oversimplification. It's intentional myopia masquerading as omniscience. Hitchens is fond of the word "solipsism." It's that.

It's also political and not only theoretical. Either Dawkins and Harris haven't thought through what they're saying or they're taking us along step by step to a destination they realize we'd avoid if we recognized it in advance.

Reviewers of their books haven't spotted curtailment of civil liberties as integral to their aims. It wasn't till I had repeatedly read over the quotes above, in the course of experimenting with just how I wanted to comment on them, that I began to wonder if they portend a push for top-down control of the masses by a "rational" elite?

My position is that those who speak to our good will can also speak to our reason and can lead us to a more rational and manageable world, while those who'd regard us as sub-rational beings to be intimidated and manipulated can lead us only into larger and larger clashes with less and less room to find ways of resolving them.

(It's bizarre, surely, to have to argue against rule by ideologues in America of all places, especially after all the failed totalitarian experiments of the twentieth century. Maybe it *isn't* necessary. But it's better to make the case than to be complacent and realize later that it should've been made.)

What's vital is *who* agrees with these writers or may hereafter find it expedient to. Our society's likeliest future passes through decades of both terrorism and natural disasters resulting from global warming. That may have two opposed consequences: (1) religiousness of all kinds may increase and intensify because of the suffering and uncertainty. (2) Political "realists," who already think of democratic institutions as outmoded in an overpopulated world of vanishing resources, may take the exigencies of such a time to mandate rule by the "intelligent" over us all. Rationalists also have potential allies among the enormous corporate interests that are engendering a worldwide culture of narcissism, as the only opposition to that, now that Marxism is in eclipse, comes from religions.

When challenged over their anti-freedom positioning and rhetoric, I expect these writers are going to say, "Oh, we aren't against personal freedom; we just wrote to protest religious attacks on scientific knowledge." Please recognize that that's *not* what they did. Watch them! I'd bet that they'll go after freedom of thought again, then calculatingly deny having done so, then do it, then deny, then do,—to keep the issue ambiguous so critics can't oppose them except with contested interpretations of what they've said.

I don't think most of us would abandon freedom, human rights, and democracy for rule by rationalists, especially when it's so hard to credit rationalists with thinking rationally.

Freedom has been our greatest asset because it has let us openly work out and discuss what we think on all topics, check out unpopular theories, invent and improvise and promote without anyone's permission, make the powerful obey the laws, investigate and expose official deceptions and failures, rally for changes of government policy and get them, oust Presidents and Congresses, organize into labor unions to combat oligarchic concentrations of wealth, be secure as lone dissenters, be active in political parties and all varieties of movements so as to speak for or court majorities, and live, with a measure of privacy, according to our consciences.

Nothing but freedom lets reason be heard regardless of who else is speaking.

It's through decisions democratically made that we can most adequately confront what confronts us, however bad it gets. Elections best enable us to come up with leaderships approved of by the people and embodying the right combination of forcefulness toward circumstances and sensitivity to our personal and collective autonomy and to the governmental balances and checks that protect it (continued throughout an emergency or restored as early as feasible).

IV

I don't believe most rationalists, left to themselves, would threaten our liberties and rights, just as I don't believe most fundamentalists wish to. But today, just as fundamentalists have been tempted by the promise of a theocracy, rationalists are being tempted by the promise of an atheocracy whose decisions they'd make for everyone.

Good decision-making can't thrive in a society that's hostile to the existence of multiple viewpoints, and no one should fail to see that that's the kind of society rationalists want. The orthodoxy they'd impose goes well beyond what today's science can say.

It took the monolithic culture of the Soviet Union to make the scientific views of a Lysenko, derived from wishful thinking and ideological consistency, into Russia's official genetics for a time. Had others been allowed to dispute them, it could never have happened.

We should be wary of the proposition that our militant rationalists want to use science to settle policy questions. They've an anti-empirical bias, and true science poses a threat to it. To expect self-restraint of them once they were in authority would be foolish: they don't exercise it *now*.

You can't suppress error and repress differences unless you're willing to depress thought and oppress science.

If not held answerable to the people, they'd sacrifice the right of the people to know what's going on and do something about it. That's what governments can be trusted to do if the people aren't entrusted with the means to stop them. And what that leads to predictably is more secrecy, more irrationality, more fear, spiraling downward into savagery.

It's imperative to also keep rationalists accountable in research and academic life. When science is run by ideologues we find scientists censored or shunned or fired because they question what has been thought answered or because they want to look into forbidden areas such as, in our time, the paranormal or UFOs. Those are things that scientists ought to be able to look into.

Harris, as it happens, thinks science should explore such areas. He's also mindful of and impressed by Buddhist exercises which appear to demonstrate that the mind is independent of the body. Perhaps his visceral hatred of religion will win him a bit of leeway, but he should watch out for some of his fellow rationalists who live to sniff out heresy.

What goes with performing scientifically is an applied agnosticism, enemy to all ideology, that won't resist facts if they're discomfiting or overlook what's unlooked-for. True religion, like true science, has a use for agnosticism. It's a valuable discipline to suspend judgment. Zen masters and martial arts trainers say, "Keep don't-know mind." Hindu teachers would have us expand our intuitiveness by not holding settled opinions. Any mystic will take experiences over doctrines. When not only working scientists but spiritual persons apply the agnosticism that true science must have, why can't rationalists be asked to?

It's time we remember how often science's renegades—the Copernicuses, Galileos, and Semmelweises—have turned out to be right. And it's time scientists have a legally enforceable bill of rights, so they can't be penalized for using scientific method more scrupulously or more far-seeingly than guardians of the intellectual status quo would have them do.

<h1 style="text-align:center">V</h1>

Exaggeration and misinterpretation are big guns in the rationalist arsenal. Harris: "We can no longer ignore the fact that billions of our neighbors believe in the metaphysics of martyrdom, or in the literal truth of the book of Revelation, or any of the other fantastical notions that have lurked in the minds of the faithful for millennia—because our neighbors are now armed with chemical, biological and nuclear weapons." (p.14) Rather few of our neighbors believe in the so-called martyrdom of suicide attacks, which is the only *practical* belief he cites. Otherwise he's referring to religious doctrines.

Religious doctrines are formal beliefs: ones that people ritually affirm collectively so as to get their minds into a receptive space. Harris never grasps this. He supposes that one's stated credo necessarily dictates what one does.

Not so long ago alarmists were quoting Lenin's writings,

the "holy writ" of Soviet communism, to show that the USSR
was implacably, almost superhumanly geared to take the West
under. The operating beliefs and behaviors of the Russian leadership, however, had little to do with Lenin's doctrines. They
were less ambitious and took into account many more factors.
Harris makes the same mistake today with Muslims, ransacking
the Qur'an for verses to frighten people with, paying no mind to
the verses' historical context, and imagining that faithful Muslims have no choice but to be uncritical, robot-like enactors of
the harshest interpretations of them, no matter what's going on
around them. (See the chapter on Islamia.)

Religions recognize righteous accomodation and not only
righteous struggle. Justice without humiliation for either party
is a possibility, provided we want it and try to accomplish it.
And—very important—people can be influenced favorably regardless of what they profess. Because he won't recognize these
things, Harris purveys hysteria and nudges us toward extreme
policies.

Western societies have disrespected Muslims because of traditional religious exclusivism. And traditional religious exclusivism is seized on avidly by those Muslims who resort to terrorism.
The anti-religious exclusivism of rationalists has no way of overcoming all that wrath and only adds its own to it. If our dilemma
will yield to anything, it may to generous and intelligent attitudes
inspired by the allorance taught in all of the great religions.

Harris: "Of course, one senses that the problem is simply
hopeless. What could possibly cause billions of human beings
to reconsider their religious beliefs? And yet, it is obvious that
an utter revolution in our thinking could be accomplished in a
single generation: if parents and teachers would merely give honest answers to the questions of every child. Our doubts about
the feasibility of such a project should be tempered by an understanding of its necessity..." (p.224) Curiously, that's as close as he
and Dennett and Dawkins get to laying out a how for the speedy
planetary transition to atheism that they insist on.

It's revealing that he thinks teachers and parents aren't giving honest answers now. The inability to see beliefs dissimilar to one's own as sincere betrays a paucity of sympathetic imagination that makes productive dialogue improbable.

Harris: "A belief is a lever that, once pulled, moves almost everything else in a person's life." (p.12) That depends on what kind of belief it is and what role we want it to play. Americans have no trouble believing even contradictory things—for example that we must obey God and that the people should rule—because we believe them in different ways and to different degrees and from different motives. That leaves us room to maneuver, re-think, and re-prioritize.

If you consult David McCullough's biography, Truman, you can read what some of Harry Truman's early beliefs were as regards "Niggers," "Wops," "Kikes," "Japs," and "Chinamen." Because of those beliefs an onlooker of the Harris type might've expended great energy to keep Truman from rising politically. Yet he had no driving meanness in him. He got along with all kinds of people, supported the New Deal because he thought it humane and right, and as a U.S. Senator worked on behalf of civil rights, making it a priority once he was President although those around him were calling that political suicide. So not all of his beliefs were levers that moved everything else in his life.

And his religious turn of mind, although he said little about it, attuned him to his own better possibilities. What he believed religiously may've been typical of his place and time, but what he personally made of those beliefs grew and balanced in him virtues such as humility, gratitude, sympathy, patience, honesty, firmness, justness, and moral courage. *They* were what moved almost everything in his life.

With Harry Truman in mind, we can say that the way to get religious people to behave ideally is to appeal to what's ideal in their religions. Attack the religions themselves and you put the people on the defensive and make them cleave all the more stubbornly to the worst, most eccentric and inallorant things that they've come to think.

VI

I want to move on to Hitchens now. His book is the most erudite and culturally informed of the four. He's the sensitive soul who writes after revealing what he thinks of religion: "I trust that if you met me, you would not necessarily know that this was my view. I have probably sat up later, and longer, with religious friends than with any other kind." (p.11) Yet he's also the bully who chose that deliberately obnoxious title and subtitle: god is Not Great and How Religion Poisons Everything. I can only surmise that he's torn.

Without noticing, Hitchens gets at cross-purposes to his thesis that it's *religion* that "poisons everything." He writes: "Past and present religious atrocities have occurred not because we are evil, but because it is a fact of nature that the human species is, biologically, only partly rational." (p.8) If the problem is human nature, then the problem isn't religion. Religion does nothing. We do things. What we take from it comes down to what we want from it.

Hitchens and the others have demonstrated by what they've written that belief in reason isn't sufficient on its own to create benignity and fair-mindedness in people. If anything can do so dependably, it may be what has done so on many occasions: the intent practice of religion, not at its usual but at its best.

Unlike his three brethren, Hitchens doesn't believe it's possible to do away with religion in the near term: "Sigmund Freud was quite correct to describe the religious impulse, in The Future of an Illusion, as essentially ineradicable until or unless the human species can conquer its fear of death and its tendency to wishful thinking. Neither contingency seems very probable." (p.247) And: "Religious faith is, precisely *because* we are still-evolving creatures, ineradicable." (p.12, italics in original) If religion is a major influence and isn't about to disappear, then I'd imagine the sane thing to do would be to make it as positive an influence as we can, not to insult and maul people for being religious.

Hitchens: "The mildest criticism of religion is also the most radical and the most devastating one. Religion is man-made."

(p.10) But I've just quoted him as saying religion is "ineradicable." It can't be both too deeply rooted in us to be extracted and a mere human contrivance. Let me provide the necessary distinction. It's religions, not religion, that that are man-made (which isn't to say made in the absence of higher awareness). We're born with an inclination to be religious, as we are with inclinations to procreate, to have friends, to better our circumstances, etc. We might begin to ask whether the features that make up true religion—heightening, allorance, infinintention—come to us from evolution, or whether they're of the nature of consciousness itself, exemplifying an inherent tendency in it to the unifying, overcoming, and perfecting of what it manifests? Right now we can't say.

Rationalists think religion came into being to quell our anxieties and so is traceable to our fearfulness and self-interestedness. If they're implying that it's nothing more, that represents what's known in logic as the genetic fallacy: the idea that a thing is only what it began as (Abraham Lincoln was nothing but a rail-splitter, etc.). Our profound involvement in religious devotion and practices not only can hedge our selfishness and smallness but can outright reverse them. How religion began is both irrelevant and uncertain. We can't reduce it to those all-too-human traits when it can exist, and be most completely itself, without them.

Hitchens: "(Religion) may speak about the bliss of the next world, but it wants power in this one." (p.17) Really? Did the Buddha, who walked away from a princely life to become a mendicant, want power? Did Jesus, who never made a political move? Did even Muhammad, a strong but meek man who had authority and command thrust on him thanks to his religion's enemies? Did Rama, who cheerfully agreed to fourteen years of forest exile in place of the throne that should have been his, so that his father could keep his word? These and others like them are religion's heroes and so are windows for us into what it is.

Hitchens and the others make much of religious activism against abortion and gays. Being religious doesn't imply taking those stands. Allors don't condemn homosexuality/lesbianism but would have sexuality of all kinds downplayed in our lives and eventually eliminated from them in favor of devotionality. I don't know of any allor who has commented on abortion, apart from Mother Meera's expressed unwillingness to see it made un-lawful.

Hitchens writes of two recent spiritual personalities who are known worldwide—Rajneesh (pp.195-8) and Sathya Sai Baba (pp.75-6, 195)—as representing what the East has to offer, of which he doesn't think much. But anyone familiar with their careers should be disinclined to regard either as a genuine allor. The earlier Sai Baba, the saint of Shirdi, whose reincarnation Sathya Sai says he is and who remains extravagantly popular in India, would be far harder to discount and isn't mentioned. Hitchens makes it too easy for himself.

Hitchens: "Religion comes from the period of human prehistory where nobody—not even the mighty Democritus who concluded that all matter was made from atoms—had the smallest idea what was going on." (p.64) But *now* we know? If so, how is matter related to consciousness? Science so far hasn't been able to tell us. And that's basic! Until we have the answer to that, the true dynamics of everything remain indefinite to us. We can't say whether we have materialism, or idealism, or something else.

The answer to that could provoke a crisis for rationalism, which hinges on unproved beliefs about how things are. True religion, however, hinges on receptiveness/infinintention and so isn't at war with any fact.

Hitchens: "The search for nirvana, and the dissolution of the intellect, goes on. And wherever it is tried, it produces a Kool-Aid effect in the real world." (p.198) So the Buddha and his disciples committed mass suicide? And Zen masters are without intellect? And there's no reason to consider Nirvana attainable? Going by the evidence, I'd have to disagree.

Hitchens, in a chapter titled "Is Religion Child Abuse?": "How can we ever know how many children had their psychological and physical lives irreparably maimed by the compulsory inculcation of faith?" (p.217) With real faith, which can't be imposed on people, that doesn't happen. And it could just as plausibly be argued that it's child abuse in this dreadfully difficult world to deny children the peace of mind, the allorance, and the heightening that come with true religion and which often they can absorb more readily than adults can.

"(M)y parents' faith was so persuasively transmitted by contagion rather than by coercion that I recall in my childhood no revolt against it, only a cordial acceptance and a sensitive response." The quote is from the autobiography of Harry Emerson Fosdick, a famed Protestant clergyman of the twentieth century (The Living of These Days (New York, Harper ChapelBooks, 1956, p.19) That's how it should, and sometimes does, go in our homes.

My own religious upbringing was in mainstream Protestantism, which I felt to be neither toxic nor as nourishing as it might've been. Although Christianity is no longer my religion, I continue to cherish the inducements to allorance and heightening that I was introduced to in it. Never did I attend a pogrom, burn someone at the stake, fight in a holy war, or fly an airplane into a skyscraper. Did I miss what religion is for? Or has Hitchens?

He has written an unflattering book about Mother Teresa, lewdly titled The Missionary Position (Verso, 1995). He sees her as a fanatic who lived to promote Catholicism (although the order she founded doesn't proselytize and her views weren't exclusivistic). While I don't think the acclaimed nun was an allor, much of her behavior was allorant, which can't be said for him.

Time Magazine for September 3, 2007 had a cover article about her (vol. 170 no. 10, pp.36-41), including comments by Hitchens that display the familiar rationalist disrespect, intolerance, and refusal to stop and think. The article discusses the contents of the new book, Mother Teresa: Come Be My Light (Mother Teresa and Brian Kolodiejchuk, Doubleday, 2007), which makes public for the first time certain of her letters and writings. These, says the article, "reveal that for the last nearly half-century of her life she felt no presence of God whatsoever—or, as the book's compiler and editor, the Rev. Brian Kolodiejchuk writes, 'neither in her heart or in the eucharist.'" (p.38)

Hitchens, typically, jumps on that without the least allowance for doubt or alternate possibilities as to what it might signify.

The article quotes him as saying: "She was no more exempt from the realization that religion is a human fabrication than any other person, and that her attempted cure was more and more professions of faith could only have deepened the pit that she had dug for herself." (pp.38-9) But her discouragement and "dryness" don't equate with her seeing through a falseness of religion. Aren't there scientists who've likewise become depressed and had to battle a sense of futility about the basic meaningfulness of their careers for years or decades? Does that make science a fraud? And does he really think she was more insightful than all the nuns and priests who are able to live and function in relative mental peace?

"In 1948, Hitchens ventures, Teresa finally woke up, although she could not admit it," the article states. "He likens her to die-hard Western communists late in the cold war: 'There was a huge amount of cognitive dissonance,' he says. 'They thought, "Jesus, the Soviet Union is a failure, [but] I'm not supposed to think that. It means my life is meaningless." They carried on somehow, but the mainspring was gone. And I think once the mainspring is gone, it cannot be repaired.' That, he says, was Teresa." (p.41) (He also reviewed the book in the *Newsweek* of September 10, 2007.)

I want to continue this with an

OPEN LETTER TO CHRISTOPHER HITCHENS:

Sir,

Show you a sad and anxious nun and you'll say she woke up. Show you a merry and contented nun and you'll say she's asleep. If you'd put aside your animus for a moment, you'd recognize that that's all tendentiousness and that you haven't proved a thing.

According to you, Mother Teresa was in denial. Was she?

Or are you? For you don't ask the logical question. That is: Why would she have *expected* to feel the presence of God in the first place? Here's why. She was aware that there are people who feel it all the time. And the article's reference to her not having felt it in almost fifty years brings out that she had felt it previously.

If some people experience what's called the presence of God, then there's nothing irrational about wanting to experience it. And when you use waking up as a metaphor for ceasing to have that experience, you yourself generate "cognitive dissonance."

I don't attempt to say what the presence of God is, whether it's what the name asserts or something else; but it's a known phenomenon. Many of us who pray, I think, have had a taste of it, however fleetingly. For some it's so powerful and enduring that there's no way they can be said to have psyched themselves into it. What we psych ourselves into lasts only so long, till it runs up against something contrary. An experience such as this that can be permanent isn't like being brainwashed, because it harmonizes our nature rather than splitting it.

Religion is nobody's fabrication. It often enters our lives unbidden. It's more real and more mysterious than the rest of what we encounter. How long you can keep that recognition at bay, clinging to rationalist illusions like oldtime communists clinging to the disintegrating USSR, is past guessing.

Even if you had gotten Mother Teresa right, there are and have been greatly greater spiritual personages at large in the world. If you honestly wish to help us think about religion instead of childishly venting at it, you might write a detailed, thoughtful, nuanced, *unbiased* essay on an allor about whom we're well informed: say, Anandamayi Ma or Swami Vivekananda.

Your undertaking that would afford you fresh material and let you be intriguingly inconsistent and philosophically deeper. The alternative would seem to be that you go on to exhaust the public's patience with your anti-religious diatribes.

But I caution you: if you dare to go ahead with such a biography, you'll be changed by it.

-John Gibson

All of these writers proclaim rationalists to be (at least potentially) as moral as anyone. From what they write about themselves, they're a pretty self-satisfied lot. They think the value of our existence is in what we do for society, so they don't try to inculcate higher inward traits in themselves.

Nor do they consider that doing that might help them to help society by augmenting their insightfulness and their character and therefore augmenting the appeal that character and insightfulness can bestow, to the benefit of their influence.

They're very conventional, too, not inclined to be dissatisfied with the bourgeois valuations and the ethical indifference of our contemporary society.

A living allor embodies a keenly intelligent social critique that you can learn from and emulate. If you start out thinking no one could possibly be more moral than your own cohort, how morally alert are you going to be?

Not in his book but at different times Hitchens has asked rhetorically what religious people can do that secular people can't? I'll answer with reference to an early twentieth century figure, Maria Goretti, and the people around her. She was declared a saint by the Catholic church because of what she naturally did that most people could never bring themselves to do.

Beautiful and mature for her age, which was twelve, the very religious Maria was stabbed to death by a nineteen-year-old neighbor who had tried to rape her. Before she died she told people that she wanted her killer, Alessandro Serenelli, to join her in heaven. He lied about the crime and was defiant; but when he began his long prison sentence with three months of enforced solitude, the gravity of what he had done got through to him and he became truly remorseful and took on new qualities. He later related that he had had a dream during this time in which Maria stood before him and handed him fourteen white lilies, one after another: one for each time he had stabbed her. After his eventual release he went to Maria's mother, Assunta, and asked her forgiveness. She adopted him as her son. For the rest of his eighty-eight years he lived devoutly as a gardener for the Capuchins. In old age, having learned the anatomy of going wrong and going right, he offered a statement that included the words, "I feel that religion with its precepts is not something we can live without, but rather is the real comfort, the real strength in life and the only safe way in every circumstance..." (Full statement quoted at http://www.mariagoretti.org/alessandro.htm.)

Now, what can religious people, or more precisely those who practice true religion wholeheartedly, do that secular people can't? Through devotion they can become so inwardly free, impartial, and mentally at peace as to gladly rescue even their mortal enemies. They can affect others favorably to a degree that's incomparable. Sometimes they can turn a debauched predator who'd rape a child into a person of integrity who's firmly ready to protect the innocent and give help to whoever needs it. They can become humanly superlative.

Nothing but religion acts in us at such depths.

To be transformed doesn't occur minus the conceptual opening to something beyond one's own perceptible bounds, whether that be a being or a state of being. Secularists therefore have no means of aspiring to it and must deride it or deny its existence.

Look around you. The world is full of violence, accompanied by emotional trauma. Victims who could be any of us die with fear and hate and self-pity, but Maria didn't. Criminals live with guilt and denial and resentment, but Alessandro didn't. Survivors become outraged and bitter and vengeful, but Assunta didn't. What if many, many more of us longed and strove for the ability to be people of the sort who can give and accept forgiveness as deeply as these few did and thus be released from painful and haunting negativity, always without countenancing wrongdoing? The society would be altered because the rest of the people would see something more inspiring as possible *for* themselves and so could demand more *of* themselves.

That won't happen if our culture's standard-setters believe, despite the contrary evidence, that our low-quality responses to our lives' afflictions are inevitable and so unsurpassable.

Initially Alessandro blamed Maria for his lustful and murderous actions because of his attraction to her. A Hitchens will blame religion for his rage because of his hatred for it, refusing to take responsibility for his own inflamed emotions and words. Rationalists think everything is objectively determined, which is why they're reactive. Maria and Assunta were able to experience the world as having only a relative and ambiguous existence, not as the prime reality. Because their lives were centered subjectively in the higher, for them to live was to expand into peaceful space rather than to run up against a pernicious human nature in themselves that was controlled by the behavior of others.

What they did, any of us can do who surpassingly wants to.

VII

On to Dennett now for the first time.

He's superficially unlike the others, coming across as reasonable and adult, if verbose. He's avuncular, witty, mildly condescending, slightly unctuous. He sometimes presents himself as sympathetic to religious people, in a patronizing way.

He has a professor's overly thorough style of presentation. As we'll see below, he departs from it with procedural moves that are to rationalism's advantage and not to that of science.

He calls for scientific study of religion's origins. The research he wants is anticipated to reveal religious beliefs and behaviors as traceable to evolutionary factors. The confirmation that we've evolved into religion would no doubt be devastating to fundamentalism. But he doesn't ask if there's a kind of religion to which it's innocuous. Shouldn't he, since there is?

Rejecting William James' concentration on the individual, Dennett says he wants to view religion socially and biologically and so will write about groups. As for the religious individual: "(J)ust as James could hardly deny the social and cultural factors, I could hardly deny the existence of individuals who very sincerely and devoutly take themselves to be the lone communicants of what we might call private religions. Typically these people have had considerable experience with one or more world religions and have chosen not to be joiners. Not wanting to ignore them, but needing to distinguish them from the much, much more typical religious people who identify themselves with a particular creed or church that has many members, I shall call them *spiritual* people, but not *religious*." (p.11)

He assumes that those who are interiorly religious have private religions and don't participate in the established ones. Based on what? (No footnotes, no explanation.) He reclassifies them as spiritual and thereby severs them from his investigation, even invoking them by implication *against* religions. By what right? They're the ones who are the most fruitfully religious, for heightening is an individual and not a group event.

Everything higher in religious practice is spiritual, though not everything in religions is. "I'm spiritual, not religious" signifies "I do religious-type things but am not confined to a religion." A peeling away of the spiritual from the religious serves only to reduce what we mean by "religion" to what's lower in it.

What Dennett's studies won't do, then, is to consider the signal improvements that can take place in religious persons. His methodology is indefensible because there can't be an adequate overview of religion that leaves aside the ways in which individuals, as such, are affected by practicing it.

He says nothing about allors. If he doubts that such persons have existed, why doesn't he look and see if they're here now? How could the growing of exceptionally great and good persons in religious life tell us nothing about its nature and its potential? Why instead would he want to understand it in terms of ordinary congregations and what makes them dull and unreasoning?

Dennett offers a "tentative" definition of what religions are: *"social systems whose participants avow belief in a supernatural agent or agents whose approval is to be sought."* (p.9, italics in original) If we went along with that, it'd follow that Buddhism, Jainism, Daoism, Confucianism, Advaita Vedanta, and Unitarianism-Universalism *aren't* religions. But everyone agrees that they are.

In the first chapter I defined religion as beyonding, which makes religions examples of that. To beyond, I said, is "to relate oneself to what one conceives to exceed the psychological and material bounds we're all familiar with in the interest of one's being made more satisfactory." Would Dennett deny that that's what religion is? It's a definition that fits *all* of the larger religions, while Dennett's omits a third if not half of them.

Is the objective existence of the "supernatural agent" the crux of the matter for him? As I noted in the first chapter, the higher has to be sought through heightening, subjectively. Pursuing it objectively is like trying to reach the top of a mountain by descending into its valley. Dennett should have foreseen that, at least as how things might be.

And his formula seizes on propitiation as the purpose of religion. That may be the doctrine most familiar to his readers, but what of the rest of humanity? There are religions premised on how we can please God or gods. There are religions premised on how we can live according to nature. There are religions premised on how we can be happy. A shoe-horn is not a scientific instrument.

He'd have religions seen as uniform and theistic. He quotes two authors (pp.197-8) who report that only small elites hold to godlessness within even nominally godless religions such as Buddhism and Jainism. The point for an intelligent scholar isn't how many subscribe to a type of religion such as the theistic or the non-theistic, but what effect their practice of it can have on them.

He asks rhetorically, "(I)f the 'elites' find that they just cannot bring themselves to 'believe they have experienced long and satisfying exchange relations with' God, why do they persist with (something they call) religion at all?" (p.198) Is there nothing in religions to attract people apart from beliefs about God? And if something isn't theistic, can't it be religious all the same?

What the major religions have in common, as Dennett could've discovered, is not theism but some form of devotion plus infinintention, allorance, and heightening. Theism represents one possible theme invoked to produce devotion and allorance. Its role can be displaced by, for example, meditation or a monism that's a rationale for love of all beings.

Our society is more and more disparate in its religious forms. Valid conclusions about religion over-all can't be acquired from observations about only theism, let alone about only collective worship in the main sects of the monotheist traditions. What's the scientific value of ethnocentrism?

Dennett: "My focus...on Christianity first, and Islam and Judaism next, is unintended but unavoidable: I simply do not know enough about other religions to write with any confidence about them." (pp.xiii-iv) Ignorance is a peculiar criterion for scientific sampling, I'd think. Why not do the research instead of using a too-small database?

He introduces into his discussion the fanciful eschatological beliefs of cargo cults (pp.98-100). (So do Dawkins, his pp.202-7, and Hitchens, his pp.155-8.) That *might* be a sly way of caricaturing religion and insinuating that it's primitive and ridiculous. When Dennett is willing to devote space to a topic as fatuous as cargo cults, what excuse has he for omitting (a) non-dogmatic, experienced-based religions which conspicuously require the use of intelligence, such as Daoism, Sufism, Advaita Vedanta, and Buddhism, and (b) the actual thinking of many good and unpretentious worshipers in the religions he has chosen to concentrate on, who employ beliefs devotionally and *not* as factual claims and points of contention against other religions and the sciences?

If the problem of religion as Dennett sees it is that it suppresses reason with "faith," how can he be impervious to the kinds of religion that don't do that? And mightn't replacing irrational strains of religion with rational strains be more practicable than trying to get humanity to indiscriminately forsake all religions, when religion has such magnetism for so many?

Dennett: "It is time for the reasonable adherents of all faiths to find the courage and stamina to reverse the tradition that honors helpless love of God—in any tradition. Far from being honorable, it is not even excusable. It is shameful." (p.298) The context of this pronouncement is a discussion of religious tyranny and terrorism. Where did the idea come from that these reflect "helpless love of God"? I think most of us think of the true lovers of God as the true lovers of humanity. People like Francis of Assissi and Abraham Joshua Heschel come to mind. Wherein is that mistaken? We aren't told, and I don't think we will be.

It's difficult to believe that Dennett has any interest in religions except for how to depopulate them. He's unjustifiably selective. He doesn't examine religion as a whole to determine its range of major expressions and their possibilities. He declines to take up what all religions at their best include. Referring to a theologian's wish to exempt religious phenomena from scientific judgment, he deplores the "cherry-picking" of evidence as "a scientific sin." (p.364) It's one he himself is maximally guilty of.

Why can't he ask for a real and comprehensive investigation of what religion is? Because it could be time-consuming and in too many ways inconclusive. He's in a hurry to move the world away from religion. That doesn't go with writing objectively and reasonably about it.

I'll end this section with an

OPEN LETTER TO DANIEL C. DENNETT:

Sir,

You (p.21), abetted by Dawkins (his p.338) and others, are campaigning to have rationalists, and no one else, called "brights." I don't see why anyone would concur. Socrates and other well-known religious people have been exceedingly bright. Why can't you admit as much?

Hitchens on his p.5 calls this self-glorification of yours "cringe-making." It also tells us what we can look forward to from you.

You write: "Maybe in the future, if more of us brights will just come forward and calmly announce that of course we no longer believe in any of those Gods, it will be possible to elect an atheist to some office higher than senator." (p.245) Not with *that* attitude it won't.

Do you really think the people admire your contempt for their devotionality and your sense of superiority and entitlement? Maybe you should go into politics and see.

When Hitler came to power, scientists flocked to him, eager

to be rid of the old restraints and to engineer a new humanity through racial culling and eugenics. They dreamed of a world where tolerance and respect could be denied to the weak, the "inferior," and the ones unlike themselves. I don't believe you share their racism, but I also don't believe you'd ordain that the religious or people with IQs below your own should have a voice equal to yours in our political system, assuming you'd allow them any at all.

Tell me I'm wrong if you can.

-John Gibson

VIII

Now back to Harris: "The Holocaust...is generally considered to have been an entirely secular phenomenon. It was not. The anti-Semitism that built the crematoria brick by brick --- and that still thrives today—comes to us by way of Christian theology. Knowingly or not, the Nazis were agents of religion." (p.79) While I agree with the preceding remark, note that incredible last one! The logic of it lumps everyone religious in with friends of genocide.

I suppose he'd argue that being religious means opposing reason and therefore being capable of ruinous behaviors. How can anyone fail to see that one can be both religious and rational? One can resort to religion precisely for the most rational of reasons: so as to undergo heightening and thereby come to be a higher, wiser, freer, and more natural human being, one who can be happy and of truer value to everyone.

We can even ask whether one can be convincingly rational and *not* seek to be heightened?

To him, Nazis and religious people occupy the same niche. But as far as that goes, you might ask yourself who'd be *less* disposed to send you to a death camp: someone intemperate, inflexible, intolerant, and too-clever, like Harris, or a Muslim or Christian cleric who respects others' religions, appeals to allorance, and works patiently for justice and peace? There are plenty of both types around, so choose well. One day you may have to.

Harris: "Moderates in every faith are obliged to loosely interpret (or simply ignore) much of their canons in the interest of living in the modern world...The first thing to observe about the moderate's retreat from scriptural literalism is that it draws its inspiration not from scripture but from cultural developments that have rendered many of God's utterances difficult to accept as written." (p.17) Again: "The only reason anyone is 'moderate' in matters of faith these days is that he has assimilated some of the fruits of the last two thousand years of human thought (democratic politics, scientific advancement on every front, concern for human rights, an end to cultural and geographic isolation, etc.) The doors leading out of scriptural literalism do not open from the inside." (pp.18-19) Wrong. And, by the way, can this extoller of "the fruits of the last two thousand years" be the atavistic absolutist who'd deny people the use of their personal judgment about religion?

Many religious people have reluctantly retreated to tolerance, yes; but others, in all historical periods, have been allorant rather than sectarian. Indifference to our differences is characteristic of allors and good everyday religious people who don't hunger for strife or dominion. We see it, for example, in the Muslims in Rwanda who rescued Christian Tutsis from the genocide there.

Harris would insinuate that the moderate and the allorant are responding to community opinion and not to their religions. But it's the allorant who respond to what's essential in their religions more directly and completely than anyone else does. And the modern developments he writes of had many sponsors and even inaugurators among religious moderates at every level, or they couldn't have come about in societies where a church was the decisive institution and most educated people supported it.

Harris: "By failing to live by the letter of the texts, while tolerating the irrationality of those who do, religious moderates betray faith and reason equally." (p.21) If the scriptures are simply wrong, as Harris maintains, how can there be a right way to read them? And who is he, having denounced the scriptures and religion, to tell the religious they must go by the letter of the texts? That takes some nerve, not to mention some illogic!

Many of us see the authenticity of a religious life in its greatness of soul, not in literal-mindedness. What's wrong with heightening as the criterion of religious truth? Allors and allorists have *always* gone beyond the letter of the texts. And they discern much more in the texts than literalists can.

Far from betraying reason and faith as Harris says they do, the finest people affirm their faith and their reason together by lowering themselves before the higher and trusting in the best that comes from their hearts and their heads when they read their scriptures and worship. That's often how true religion is begun!

Here's Dennett again: "As Sam Harris argues...there is a cruel catch-22 in the worthy efforts of the moderates and ecumenicists of all religions: by their good works they provide protective coloration for their fanatical co-religionists, who quietly condemn their open-mindedness and willingness to change while reaping the benefits of the good public relations they thereby obtain." (p.299) I'd have thought it was the other way around: that the extremists give the moderates a bad name. At any rate, that's what Dennett and Harris are plainly bent on causing to happen.

Dennett: "Any vicious cult that uses Christian imagery or texts as its protective coloration should lie heavily on the conscience of all who call themselves Christians...Until the priests and rabbis and imams and their flocks explicitly condemn *by name* the dangerous individuals and congregations within their ranks, they are *all* complicit." (p.301, italics in original) Anyone who thinks about it can recognize what mischief there is in this attribution of the widest possibly complicity in wrongs, and how self-serving it is for a proselytizing rationalist like Dennett to propose it.

Moreover, it's a short step from dictating what the consciences of religious people should compel them to do, to dictating what society should compel them to do. To demand that people denounce something—anything—reeks of fascism.

All members of a religion are complicit unless they denounce that religion's extremists and extremist organizations by name? *How* are they complicit? Why should someone who's a loving person and a good neighbor feel constrained to denounce anyone? There are religious people who make it a discipline never to speak ill of another person. Isn't that their right?

Must an allorant Muslim denounce Islamist militants because the latter also call themselves Muslims and think they're acting for Islam? But what have they in common when it comes to what counts? Nothing! When you put it that way, you can see that what's involved here is simply guilt by association. And what's rational about that?

Of course, Dennett has in mind most Muslims and not just the allorant ones (of whom, however, there are more than a few). He appears to be subtly aligning himself with the view that all Muslims are alike and no better than the worst because they won't criticize the worst. Acceptance of that would further his anti-religion agenda—and our society's irrationality.

It's realistic to remember that most Muslims inhabit or hail from societies in which speaking out is discouraged, sometimes lethally. It isn't what they're accustomed or inclined to. That doesn't make them sympathetic to terrorism. But if anything will, it's to treat them as though they were.

And Dennett and Harris have it wrong. Those who are complicit with religious zealots aren't religious moderates but anti-religious zealots. They strengthen the two extremes by weakening those in the middle. It's on the citizens in the middle, on their peaceful instincts and their *tolerance and respect* for people who differ from them, that the justness of any society must rely.

IX

Speaking of anti-religious zealots, let's move on to Dawkins. He writes: "I am attacking God, all gods, anything and everything supernatural, wherever and whenever they have been or will be invented." (p.36)

He has repeatedly gone out of his way to offend the sensibilities of all who are religious, which includes the most inoffensive, the most giving, and the greatest in spirit and compassion and wisdom. That's the recourse of someone who's unable to distinguish real people from abstractions.

If he's "Darwin's Rottweiler," as he's being billed (T.H. Huxley was "Darwin's Bulldog"), it's time he was housebroken.

Dawkins states that gods and God were invented. The last I heard, it hadn't been demonstrated that they were. It's known that meditating Buddhists sometimes have visions of bodhisattvas and that Hindus deep in meditation have experienced deities such as Kali and Krishna. Have these divine beings been seen because we believe in them, or do we believe in them because they've been seen? Right now we have no way of knowing and can only go by what it pleases us to assume.

Since reports of "supernatural" phenomena—hauntings, poltergeists, possessions, angelic visitations, alleged past-life regressions with xenoglossy, Marian apparitions, out-of-body experiences, near-death experiences, etc.—abound, many of them from evidently credible contemporary people, it's apposite for us to explore what actually has been taking place. And some—not enough—research into that is being conducted. Shall we scrap it and refer everyone to Dawkins because his mind is made up?

He'd have "the supernatural" be regarded as apart from the natural and not as more of it. But is it, or, say, might natural laws we're not yet acquainted with apply to the "supernatural" overriding of the laws we know? Surely whether anything can accurately be termed supernatural ought to be of interest to one who denies (based on nothing) that anything exists that naturalism can't account for?

Dawkins remarks, after stating that he'll discuss the Abrahamic religions: "And I shall not be concerned at all with other religions such as Buddhism or Confucianism. Indeed, there is something to be said for treating these not as religions at all but as ethical systems or philosophies of life." (pp.37-8) There's nothing whatever to be said for it, and Dawkins can't be so ill-informed as to believe there is. I'd not be surprised if there's more to Confu-

cianism than mores. As for Buddhism: anyone with even a rudi-
mentary acquaintance with it knows that it isn't a philosophy of
life and isn't an ethical system. It's a cluster of skilled practices,
attitudes, and ways of living, designed to introduce persons into
Nirvana. And there's much compelling testimony that Nirvana is
real and attainable. Science, anyone?

Like Dennett, Dawkins is trying to define away anything religious that impinges on his ability to generalize for his own ends.
Whether any of these people even care what the truth is, is a
good question. It may be that they just want their kind of world,
run by their kind of people, and are determined to run over anyone who's in the way of their getting it.

Dawkins: "Imagine, with John Lennon, a world with no religion. Imagine no suicide bombers, no 9/11, no 7/7, no Crusades, no
witch hunts, no Gunpowder Plot, no Indian partition, no Israeli-
Palestinian wars, no Serb/Croat/Muslim massacres, no persecution of Jews as 'Christ-killers', no Northern Ireland 'troubles',
no 'honor killings', no shiny-suited bouffant-haired televangelists
fleecing gullible people of their money..." (p.1) And, after we've
somehow dispensed with the religious proclivities of billions of
people, we'll all live in a John Lennon paradise? Can he be that
credulous?

To what extent has society been harmed by religiousness as
such, and to what extent has religiousness been for wrongdoers
mainly an excuse and a rallying point, with their motives lying
elsewhere, as when greed fueled the Crusades? Hadn't we better
get more sophisticated answers to such questions before decid-
ing what religion's place in the world realistically is and exactly
what should be done with regard to it?

And is there any guarantee that the removal of religion would
result in fewer of the disasters that Dawkins cites? If human nature can wreak havoc for religion, it can wreak havoc for any
grand summation of things. The rationalist grand summation
includes, according to Harris, a "fresh moral imperative" that
religion be abolished. That may mandate, or degenerate into,
state persecution of everyone who's religious. Enthusiasts of the

French Revolution may have thought of that sort of thing as reason regnant, but I don't figure our contemporary psychologists and sociologists would.

While Dawkins goes on at length about the evils brought about by religious persons and bodies, he seems uninterested in what worldwide *benefits* there may have been from the graceful, quiet, ubiquitous practicing of religions by good human beings in tremendous numbers. Wouldn't it be more scientific to seek a way of ascertaining what the effect of true religion on a community is and can be? There's no reason experiments can't be devised for that.

Our rationalists ask for no inquiry into what the world might be like if religion were absent from it, though they have to know that any sweeping alteration of the human scene will have unintended consequences. Is that rational or reckless?

Dawkins' implicit premise is that the departure of religion would leave things unchanged except for improvements. Nietzsche, by contrast, was prepared to face unflinchingly the worst that a religionless world might present us with. He didn't giddily predict that godlessness would liberate us but warned emphatically against nihilism. He well foresaw the meaninglessness, decadence, and craziness that afflict our "advanced" societies, and he thought we must strengthen our spirits to overcome them. What if he had that right? These writers haven't thought it to the bottom.

Dawkins can't wait to get rid of God, his chosen nemesis. Whatever God's ontological status may be, God as a *concept* is humanity's symbol of supreme goodness, purity, and transformative grace. "Attacking God" signifies not a triumph of reason over superstition but a steep descent from the summit of our cultural strivings.

In his book Dawkins repeatedly characterizes what he's doing as "raising consciousness." He has that diametrically wrong. What it takes to raise consciousness is heightening. What he offers is the weighing down of minds through indoctrination.

X

The real problems of today are bad enough without inventing more. In a time of nuclear, biological, and chemical weapons, of global warming, of rapidly spreading terrorism, of diminishing potable water, of shrinking fuel supplies, of medicine-resistant bacteria and new diseases, of a deteriorating natural environment, of dislocations from overpopulation, and of disillusionment with our society's rewards and ideals, I should think we'd want to form the largest possible coalition for new practical thinking and action. Ought we to instead deliberately polarize ourselves by turning those who aren't religious against those who are? An outlook that'd have us do such wasteful and counterproductive things has to have its origin in emotion and not in reason.

Of course it's aggravating when fundamentalists use Bible verses to controvert the findings of the natural sciences, try to dictate how research must turn out, and plot to subvert the teaching of science in the public schools. But none of that excuses what Dennett, Dawkins, Hitchens, and Harris are doing. Their unfairness to religion is unfairness to their readers, who have every reason to feel betrayed and misled.

"Raising consciousness"? More like raising hackles. Three of the four—all but Dennett—discuss religion in the hyperbolic, pseudo-out-of-control style that has become fashionable lately. Its use denies that there is or should be a commons among us. Its mentality is tribal and punitive. It puts self-indulgence above the writer's justness, punctiliousness, and capacity for thoughtful deliberation. That people who claim to trust in reason should resort to it is ironic, as it dissolves rational discourse in bile and cynicism.

It can be objected, "They have a right to advocate science in their own way." But if we may no longer say anything that might reduce society's rationality, which appears to be their criterion for permissible public speech, then they *don't* have a right to do it. How can one advocate science using language and assumptions that dispose people *against* weighing things dispassionately and remaining aware, flexible, and analytical?

We've been warned now that some who think alike within our intelligentsia have no intention of being moderate, discriminating, mature, judicious, patient, measured, rounded, modest, or duly cautious in what they put before us. It's a trend that, if it accelerates, can only set up additional obstacles to a founding of constructiveness worldwide.

More immediately, it signals the erosion of a longtime consensus among us which upholds decent regard for others' views and for political institutions that don't take sides in our philosophical disputes. That that consensus should be rejected even by scientists, whose freedom of inquiry depends on it, is indicative of a growing irrationality in our society.

These four books do violence to reason. They marshal scholarship in support of propaganda. They'd recruit, not assist independent thinking. They give us intolerance, disrespect, sophistry, apriorist straitjacketings of reality, convenient blind spots, atheism where there should be agnosticism, finality where there should be provisionality, shaking-with-anger wrongheadedness, and other abrogations of what it is to be scientific and rational.

While some may view their writers as liberals and civil libertarians because they oppose theocratic tendencies and support equality for sexual minorities and the availability of abortion, we mustn't fool ourselves about that. They're a distinct breed of rightist hard-liners, as witness their elitism and their disdain for the right of those they consider inferior—that is, the "irrational" masses—to think for themselves.

Here's the heart of it: as long as rationalists believe that *they're* rational and the rest of us aren't, they'll be be a danger to the rest of us. Let's continue, then, to spell out how rationally deficient and intellectually sclerotic they in fact are.

And let's bluntly tell the megalomaniacs among them, as many times as necessary, that they're going to be held answerable to the equal human rights of all of us—not excluding the least, the lowest, and the most ignorant and superstitious.

FOUR

THE TRUEST FAITH

I

The most difficult feature of religion to get right may be faith. Working out what I say here has been more intellectually demanding than anything else in this book. And you may notice that in this chapter I'm more tentative than in the others—still not sure that I've gotten at faith centrally enough.

Of this much I've been convinced from the outset: it's not faith to say that the Hebrew Bible is divinely inspired, or that being a martyr for Allah is a conduit to paradise, or that Jesus factually rose from the dead. Those are examples of pretended knowledge, and to insist on them is to replace the humility of faith with the willfulness of fanaticism. Or, if you wish to follow the convention that judges fanaticism to be faith, then what I want to write of here is faith of a very different species.

I see three kinds of faith:

(1) We'll say the first is the fanatical belief that some teaching has to reflect a fact as opposed to being loftlore. This is what enemies of religion and even many religious people hold faith to be. But facts are for proving, not for believing in the absence of proof.

(2) The second is trust in someone to do something, as in "I have faith in God to look after my needs."

(3) The third is what I consider the truest faith. It's not trust *as such* but what trusting *essentially entails*. What is it that happens

when we trust someone to do something that matters? We relax.
We feel confident. Our spirits lift and we enjoy life.

So I'm going to call that last, truest faith "all-as-ease," or *al-laseease*.

Some will be inclined to argue that allasease isn't what comprises faith but what results from having it. I'd reply that, without allasease, to have faith would be to dare, which would be fraught with anxiety. Anxiety and faith cancel one another. If allasease is what faith *is*, as opposed to what it makes possible, then trusting becomes natural, even automatic.

Is allasease complacency? No. The complacent are indifferent to circumstances only till the circumstances go against them. The allaseaseful are indifferent to circumstances whatever way they unfold.

Both faith as trust and faith as allasease come from devotion. That's the psychology of it, as those can observe who care to. When it's what we're devoted to that's transcendently important to us, the overwhelmingness of the world recedes and our devotedness re-orients us inwardly to the outer. What frees us from that overwhelmingness is our attachment, our devotion, to something that represents the higher to us.

And, on some evidence, that doesn't degrade and may enhance our functioning in life. If you feel perfect trust in someone to take charge of what matters to you, you're able to concentrate without distraction on whatever arises and handle it with self-assurance and dispatch. Allasease has that result without necessitating the belief that someone will do something for you.

An understanding of the truest faith is shared by theistic and non-theistic religions. Buddhists, for instance, make their possession of faith manifest by living for their practice and acting in the prescribed ways with confidence, compassion, and patience, regardless of what may eventuate. When they have the truest faith, that's manifest in their doing that not effortfully but allaseasefully.

II

It's possible that one's devotedness may occasion a conviction that some given thing must subsequently occur. I don't see a surefire way to judge the legitimacy of that in general. If what the person believes will happen is improbable and does happen, the person may have had true foresight, or else may only have had a fanatical belief plus lucky guesswork. Such knowing, if it's that, is to my mind less a topic for speculation than a field for science to explore.

If we go by what I said in the previous section, the faith in God or gods to do something on our behalf is a secondary kind of faith, with faith as allasease being primary. That doesn't mean that trust is undesirable. If we trust, it increases our inner freedom. But the greatest inner freedom would seem intuitively and even by definition to encompass no external reliance.

So I'd say that the test of whether one's trust in the higher is in a given case true faith should be whether one can accept without disturbance the non-occurrence of what one has anticipated and continue to feel full devotion to the one trusted in, as in the Biblical phrase, "Though he slay me, yet will I trust him." In short, trust-in is valid if its giving way is not to alarm or dejection but to allasease.

An experience of mine bears upon one way that faith and specifics can be mutually related. I wrote down the details of it within minutes of its taking place, and before writing this I read them over so as to be sure that I've recalled them exactly.

On October 15, 2005 I prayed for the answer to a question. I should add that it's to Hindu deities that I pray. I pray to them not as alternatives to God but as expressing God, or as personifying the higher, in forms that are suitably mysterious, edifying, and endearing. When I prayed on this day it was, as it mostly is, to Sri Venkateshwara, who's widely worshiped in India but little known in the West.

I wanted to ask whether I should use a storage area in my apartment to stockpile water and food, these being perilous times. It seemed a prudent idea, but I wondered if only deficient faith would commend it?

So I began praying, addressing the deity by his several appellations. As I did so, the name "Markandeya" came to me near the beginning of the list. It came just as one's next thought always does. Markandeya isn't one of the god's names, however.

As I continued, my mind's ear heard "Markandeya" once or perhaps twice more. I realized that something out of the ordinary was going on.

After praying I went online and looked up Markandeya. I was already aware that there was an ancient work called the Markandeya Purana, but I hadn't read it or read a description of it. I was unsure whether the name belonged to a myth or to a writer of sacred texts. What I found, from several sources, was this:

A couple who lived in love of the higher had long been childless. The husband prayed to Lord Siva (God again) and requested a son. Lord Siva appeared to him and offered him the choice of a foolish son who'd live into old age or a wise and spiritual son who'd die at the age of sixteen. The man unhesitatingly chose the latter.

The son was conceived and born and was given the name Markandeya. He was indeed a high-souled person. As his sixteenth birthday approached his parents were dejected, so he decided to appeal to Lord Siva to extend his life. He prayed day and night to a Siva lingam, his arms about it. When he turned sixteen and was approached by agents of Yama, the god of death, they couldn't take him because he was always wholly absorbed in worship.

So they returned to Yama and told him of it. He went himself and found Markandeya still wrapped around the lingam in prayer. Unwilling to wait longer, Yama threw his noose—and it snared both the boy and the lingam. At this, Lord Siva burst from the lingam in fury and kicked Yama to death for his impertinence.

Because the world would get painfully out of balance without death, Lord Siva restored Yama to life. But he did so with the proviso that he was to let Markandeya be.

I at once understood the story of Markandeya to say that God is to be trusted absolutely: that God will slay even death itself for the sake of a devotee. I'd think that dramatizes, and translates into, the admonition to simply have faith, or be in allasease.

Incidentally, am I irrational to believe I received a message in these circumstances? I think I'd be irrational *not* to believe it. Does my opinion come from superstition, or from some doctrine? On the contrary, it comes from evidence.

III

By leaving my storage space empty of food and drink, I've acted out of faith in Sri Venkateshwara (=God). I emphasize that that doesn't imply that I know what's going to happen.

Am I protected against dehydration and starvation? I feel that I am. And I think I'd be ungrateful, having been vouchsafed such an assurance, to entertain doubts about it, especially when I was asking for an answer. Moreover, I expect that whatever can so alter the world as to answer me can also so alter it as to act for my well-being in other respects.

Still, what if I die as a result of not stocking up? Well, I could also starve or die of thirst no matter what precautions I took, as for example if I acquired a cache of sustenance but it was destroyed in the kind of event for the aftermath of which I had acquired it.

So again I'd say that the test of one's faith is whether one goes ahead in equanimity and unconcern for oneself—in allasease—regardless of what takes place: even if, for example, you should starve after having been sure you wouldn't.

IV

How is faith related to miracles? In my case it seems a miracle told me to have faith. In some cases one hears that a person's faith has given rise to a miracle. I'd judge that the miraculous and faith are related but that we have yet to learn the mechanics, if such there be, of how.

So let scientists look at what happens where faith and miracles intersect. Let's familiarize ourselves with this area of religion and life and probe what faith as trust and the truest faith do to and for us.

FIVE

HIGHER HUMANITY

I

It's dreadful to be alone, isn't it? The thought of sleeping by oneself and spending days isolated from friends and family produces a shudder in many. Listen to the words of our popular songs. Listen to the ad that says, "With a cell phone / You're never alone." But you may also want to listen to these words:

"...I regard my last eight months in prison as the happiest period of my life. It was then that I was initiated into that new world of self-abnegation which enabled my soul to merge into all other beings, to expand and establish communion with the Lord of All Being. This could never have happened if I had not had such solitude as enabled me to recognize my real self."

Some will be quick to object that he didn't define his terms and that we can't be sure what he was referring to because so much of what he wrote is interpretation. But what matters is that we "get" the idea behind the imagery. Being alone was for him a way to something interiorly greater, whether most of us are equipt to comprehend that or not.

Hear him again: "Inside Cell 54, as my material needs grew increasingly less, the ties which had bound me to the material world began to be severed, one after another....So long as a man is enslaved by material needs—wanting to be or to possess—nothing will ever belong to him; he will always belong to 'things.' A slave to things does not exist as a human being; only when he has ceased to need things, can a man truly be his own master and so really exist."

Of course, hermits and mystics of different traditions would agree with his observations. But other prisoners undergoing solitary confinement have gone mad or killed themselves or emerged worse than they went in.

Who was he? This person was by no means out of touch with reality, as he later proved. He was a military man and patriot who was imprisoned for his part in an assassination that was intended to help end foreign domination of his country. He was tough, smart, and practical-minded as well as idealistic.

In time he became his country's president. When he did, he had the remarkable inner freedom and courage to assume the initiative and make peace with his country's bitterly hated adversary, an achievement that might till then have appeared impossible. When at length assassins came for him at a public function, he didn't try to hide amidst the bleachers but stood at attention, greeting death with dignity and without fear. His name was Anwar el-Sadat.

Hear him again about his time in prison: "Now that I had discovered and actually begun to live in that 'new world,' things began to change. My narrow self ceased to exist and the only recognizable entity was the totality of existence, which aspired to a higher, transcendental reality. It was genuinely a conquest, for in that world I came to experience friendship with God—the only friend who never lets you down or abandons you."

The quotes are from his autobiography, In Search of Identity (New York, San Francisco, Hagerstown, London, Harper & Row, 1977, 1978, respectively pp. 85, 84-5, 85-6).

This was eminently a person of great character and intelligence, who lifted his country above its region's chronic human failings. So what he reveals of himself may be of some interest to whoever wants a comprehensive view of human nature.

It may be that few of us who are out in society and able to act as we please are as free as he was when imprisoned in isolation.

I can hear skeptics ask why we should believe such a tale. One reason is the calibre of the person who told it. Another is that there's nothing he had to gain by telling it if it wasn't true.

Relating such a thing couldn't have made him more popular in Egypt, and it must've raised speculation as to whether he was an orthodox Muslim or a heretic. The obvious reason for him to say that it happened would be that it did and that he thought people should know it.

Some, such as Harris, might protest that, while what Sadat accomplished was fine, organized religion is another matter. But isn't it likely that it was precisely his conventional religious up-bringing and the concentrated worship and devotional feelings he acquired through it that attuned him to the possibility of something higher and introduced him to a deeper inwardness? Where does our religious training and experience originate if not in organized religions?

Had Sadat been a rationalist instead of a Muslim, wouldn't he have used his time in isolation to exercise his intellect instead of going beyond intellection to seek the truth of his being with the entirety of his awareness? Can we, too, put aside lesser concerns and channel our leisure into the developing of our higher nature?

You won't find Sadat's name in the index of Harris', Dennett's, Dawkins', and Hitchens' books. What *can* they say about him? That the world would be better off if he hadn't been religious? Who'd believe that?

II

I want to go on to persons of an apparently still higher spiritual type: allors in the fullest sense.

In 1977 an old friend and I drove to Sumneytown, Pennsylvania to the Kripalu Ashram. Visiting at the time was the Indian saint for whom the ashram was named, Swami Sri Kripalvanandji, also known as Bapuji ("Revered Grandfather").

The swami's chief disciple, Amrit Desai, who founded the ashram, later had the distinction of being ousted from it by his own followers over allegations of sexual misconduct and deception. While he may've been less than advertised, his guru was another matter.

All of us at the ashram went to greet Bapuji in the afternoon. We gathered at the cottage where he was staying. We lined either side of the road, then fell in behind him and walked to the outdoor spot where he was to address us. The leader of this parade, preceding Bapuji and walking backwards so as to face him, was a boy of perhaps ten. As the boy reached us, I was surprised to see a mischievous grin on his face, as though he were sharing something humorous with another kid of his own age. A moment later, when Bapuji came into view, his attention was on the boy and he wore an identical ten-year-old's grin. He was able to be completely on the kid's wavelength.

We gathered around and Bapuji spoke. His richness of personality and his devotion to the higher made him affecting and memorable. He told us about when he first took *sanyas*—became a Hindu monk. That day began his life of wandering. While he didn't mind that, he somehow disliked the idea of having to beg. But he had given himself over to God, and he accepted begging as an indissoluble part of a monk's life.

He walked for several hours, dreading having to ask people to feed him. He came to a temple in a village and went in. Shortly, people approached and asked him to accompany him to their home and eat a meal they had prepared for a guest who, it turned out, wouldn't be coming. So he ate without begging for the food. And from that time onward circumstances never required him to miss a meal. And he *never* begged. If you belong to God, he said, it's God's responsibility to take care of you.

He told a story about a man in a party traveling on horseback. At some point the man lifted his heavy bundle, which had been riding ahead of him on the horse, onto his own head as he rode. Someone asked him what he was doing, and he said the horse had carried the bundle long enough and now he was going to give it a break and carry it himself! Bapuji said that God is like the horse: he has to carry your burden whether you do or not, so you may as well set it down.

Rationalists will naturally say that this man was just very fortunate in being able to escape begging without abandoning a way of life for which begging is requisite. Whether there's more to it than that is a question to which intelligent scientists should bring their curiosity.

Bapuji was unmistakably a very high person and was greatly beloved. He had planned to stay at the ashram for only a short time before returning to India, but the continuing response to him was so great that he remained for over three years.

III

Another remarkable spiritual person resided permanently in the United States. You can go to the internet, put in the name "Sivananda- Valentina," and read about her.

She was born in China of Russian ancestry and came as an adult to Florida, where she taught yoga. She was devoted to India's Swami Sivananda, a physician who became a renowned saint; they corresponded but never met, and he thought enough of her to confer his name on her.

It's hard to know where to begin in discussing such a person. Her spirituality was infused with a love of the arts. She was a ballerina and an actress and an artist, and her uncommon gracefulness was perhaps the thing you'd notice first about her. Accounts mention her empathy, her strength, her self-restraint, her sensitivity, her chasteness, her humility, her patience, her expressiveness, her magnetism, and her tenderness. They also describe her personality with words like "unique" and "unfathomable."

Her influence on the people around her was real. Jack Phelan, who became a devotee of hers, writes at the Light of Sivananda-Valentina website of having gone to her as a young man for yoga exercises to help his back. She talked with him briefly about art, showed him the group's sanctuary, and took leave of him with a "God bless you, Jack" that reverberated in him and started something unimaginable happening. It's not that he was in love with this older woman—he wasn't—but she inconceivably moved and unsettled him and opened him to a re-centering. He started that day, he says, as a satisfied atheist and ended it by discovering that he "loved to pray." Someone who can do that with four one-syllable words is dangerous!

At that website also are writings by others about their experiences with Sivananda-Valentina. A perceptive and eloquent example is by an elderly German woman, Freulein Gusti, who knew her for years.

The group is a non-profit organization that accepts contributions and provides free online books and audios but doesn't push its views on anyone. Its members aren't saying that no one but Sivananda- Valentina can do you any good. They're just giving the world an opportunity to know the person who means the most to them and who remains the hub of their lives well after her own lifetime.

IV

Perhaps on a par with Sivananda-Valentina are a number of the persons designated saints by the Roman Catholic church. The late Padre Pio, famed for his stigmata and the miracles associated with him, comes to mind. A glance at his picture contributes to the believability of his reputation for selflessness, self-assurance, and compassion. (To call attention to him may result in controversy, but I'll take up the question of miracles in a later chapter.)

Several allors are mentioned by Harris in his book: Buddha, Shankara, Padmasambhava, Nagarjuna, and Longchenpa (p.215). He cites them to make his point that the East is spiritually ahead of the West because faith (as he uses that expression) is solely Western. The Buddhist and Hindu figures he names were in truth most impressive. Yet he doesn't refer to comparable persons who are living presently.

I suppose it's safer for him to name ones who've passed on, so they won't embarrass him by commenting on the spuriousness of his East-West dichotomy. For true faith and the truest faith (see the fourth chapter) know no geography.

In Against Fundamentalism I listed over twenty recent or current allors whose genuineness appears to me to be established.

And we're becoming more aware of them. Today even as prosaic a source as a television newscast may acquaint us with them.

I'm not special-pleading for anyone. I feel attraction to most of the allors I'm about to discuss, but none is distinctly "my guru" and I'm not associated with the followers of any of them nor with the followers' organizations.

V

One present-day allor is Ammachi (Ah-MAH-chee), more properly Amritanandamayi Ma, known as "the hugging saint," who gives a minute or two of full attention to all who wait, in city after city, nation after nation, standing in long queues for hours to have the opportunity to meet someone who loves them without having to have a reason to.

Five feet tall, she's simple in the best sense and cheerful and tireless, often keeping on the go for twenty hours a day, traveling and hugging and blessing people. Her fame is growing, her charities multiplying and expanding, her already large following increasing. Many are moved, sometimes to tears, by their encounters with her.

And someone so giving and unsparing of herself, and so intelligent in what she says, is hard to knock. If there's something to this business of religion, you'd have to predict that persons like her would exist who'd show us just what that is.

I met Ammachi in New York City in 1999. There was a large gathering in a church, and she spoke to us briefly through a translator. She told a joke about a kid who prayed that God would make China the capital of America because that's the answer he gave on a test. Her point was that we should work at changing our ways of responding to the outer world, rather than running from it or trying to impose our will on it. Then there was music for an hour and Ammachi got into it, singing, raising her arms, and calling out, sometimes with an almost laugh-like vibrato.

She can sit and smile and do nothing and still be a large presence.

Finally we each had our moment with Ammachi. She was for-

ty-four, but face-to-face she looked sixty to me, and I wouldn't
have recognized her. You kneel and put your head against her
right shoulder. She places her arm around you and chants something repetitious in her light but husky voice. She seemed to finish; but maybe she thought I needed more, as she resumed the
contact and the chanting before I could leave. Then she smiled
and pressed a Hershey's Kiss and a flower petal into my hand,
and it was someone else's turn.

VI

A comparable individual is Sri Sri Ravi Shankar, an ascetic
and teacher whose mood is contagiously ecstatic.

He visits thirty or more countries each year, and he's worth
hearing. His counsel on how to extricate ourselves from emotional enslavement is compelling; it isn't the same old nostrums.
Reading his words changes my mood for the better every time. I
met him also in New York in 1999.

Quite a few of us were gathered in an auditorium, and he arrived as we were chanting. He pranced down the aisle, grinning
and freely waving his hands above his head. It was a bit comical,
as he surely intended. The lightheartedness was infectious, and it
readied us for participation. As he spoke he frequently tossed his
head back in silent laughter, his own best audience.

At the time he was forty-three and was becoming well-known
for his Art of Living Foundation, which teaches meditation, including courses in prisons, and helps the poor through various
programs. Today he's also involved in trying to bring peace to Sri
Lanka, as some have requested him to do so.

Sri Sri is short but otherwise of average dimensions, with long
hair and a full beard and a face that hints at sensitivity, brains,
and good humor. His voice is a penetrating but pleasant tenor,
and he has a strong accent but nothing sing-song in his delivery.
His skin is rather light; his hair was jet black then but is graying
now.

He led us through some meditation exercises, then took
questions—responsively but not overly seriously. An adequate

answer, he noted, makes us think "Yes!" And since we already know that the essence of the answer is yes, why bother to ask questions?

We laughed, but he was making a point that he makes repeatedly in a number of ways: that we unwisely cling to concepts, always externalizing and intellectualizing instead of drawing the feeling of what we love into ourselves and concentrating on *that.* Doing the latter, he says, makes us emotionally independent of the outer world even while we're dealing with it efficiently.

"What is the purpose of pain?" someone inquired. He replied that we get "spaced out" when we're happy, and that pain causes us to focus. It's when we meditate, he said, that we experience concentration and happiness both at once.

"How can we forgive our parents?" someone, sadly, wanted to know. "Why forgive them?" he asked in return. Forgiving them puts them in the wrong, he said, but those who harm us are themselves victims of illusion. Forgiveness can never be total, he added, but compassion can.

He was asked how we can kill the ego. Why kill it? was his rejoinder. I didn't note down his exact wording, but this is close to it: You've been trying to kill the go for years and haven't succeeded. Why not befriend it instead? Don't worry about the ego.

Someone wished to know why he grows his hair so long. It grows on its own, he explained, and he hasn't fertilized or harvested it.

At the end of the evening Sri Sri stood on the stage and greeted his audience, which was largely Western and tended to be white and middle-aged. He hugged each of us. These were quick standing embraces, expressions of affection and not the lengthier and more elaborate contacts that Ammachi confers.

I'd estimate that, surprisingly, a good eighty percent of the people tried to touch his feet, which in India is the greatest expression of reverence. There were only a few whom he permitted to do so. Most often he intercepted them, grasping their shoulders as they bent and smilingly pulling them up into his embrace.

(Maybe they should've started back farther and dived?) He did something personal in each instance, even if it was trivial. After my hug he looked in my eyes and quietly asked, "How are you?" Up close he looked his age, and a deeper persona showed through that was grave and sympathetic.

I've heard wonderful stories about Sri Sri from people who know him. One of them spent time at his ashram and conceived a strong wish to take a walk alone with him. That seemed impossible, as everyone crowded around him and tagged along if he went anywhere. But shortly after that, Sri Sri asked this man to accompany him on a walk, and all along the way people waved and smiled but didn't come near. That kind of thing is far from unknown where allors are concerned.

VII

Other living spiritual figures who give strong evidence of being authentic allors include (but aren't confined to) Mother Meera and Swami Chidananda Saraswati (also called Muniji).

Anandamayi Ma (spelled variously) was a twentieth century allor renowned for her holiness. The name means something like "Mother of Bliss" or "Bliss-Permeated Mother," and it describes her well. From all accounts she was exceptionally aware and many exceptional things happened in her vicinity.

The Jillellamudi Mother was a twentieth century allor who lived as a housewife and mother of three in India. People even from the West came to her unbidden and without her having a publicity operation. An excellent biography of her is Richard Schiffman's Mother of All (San Diego, Blue Dove Press, 2001). Schiffman spent considerable time with her and was able to describe the ordinariness of life in her home and the extraordinariness of what occurred in the people around her.

She was someone you could chat with like the mother of a friend, yet she was also capable of saying, "I see divinity in all of you, and you see human nature in me." "I don't know anything; I know everything." "I am not God and you are not the devotees; I am not the guru and you are not the disciples; I am not the guide and you are not the pilgrims. I am the Mother and you are the children."

VIII

In Meher Baba we have an allor whose status is often disputed because thinking about him blows people's minds.

A rationalist could point to all sorts of seemingly discrediting information about him, things that could suggest he was insane or a spectacular impostor, though there was never anything sexual or otherwise exploitative in what he did. So with him you have to be careful not to reach hasty conclusions. To look at his pictures, read his words, and let yourself be intuitive may be the best way to get a sense of him.

The main thing to understand about Meher Baba is that many were irresistibly drawn to him because, although he sometimes put them through trials and difficulties, he constantly and implicitly gave them love that made all the difference to their lives. Sometimes he was puzzling, but always he was devoted to them and to their ability to be heightened. And he clearly knew what he was doing, even if they didn't.

When you see photos of his large features it may strike you as incongruous that his devotees frequently have written that he was "beautiful" and "lovely" in appearance. But maybe their eyes were more educated than other people's. And there are many descriptions of the liveliness and expressiveness of his face, his hands, his body. You get the idea of acute sensitivity that translated into higher artistry.

Baba referred to himself as "the Avatar, the Ancient One, the Highest of the High." (Gore Vidal incorporated that phrase into his novel Kalki, about a fake but fateful messiah, which I take to mean that he couldn't improve on it.) Baba said that he had taken birth previously as great religious figures such as Krishna, the Buddha, Jesus, and Muhammad. He didn't demand that people believe these claims, but he repeatedly made them.

All of this was too much for quite a few, because it went

against their impression of how the world is, and perhaps because
it seemed to them to be sensationalistic, grandiose, gaudy.

Others didn't know what to make of it but were so enamored
of him that they didn't care. It perhaps served, for one thing, as a
test of who'd be steady in their adherence to him and who'd give
way because of appearances or fear of ridicule.

Without question I'd entertain versions of how things are
that are contrary to what he said. Yet I also find that the act of
rejecting what he said would make me feel that I had slapped his
face, an idea that repels me because I revere him. And I can see
it may be that his words have some kind of appropriateness to
them, even if not the obvious kind. They tell of that "majesty in
servitude" that was his motto.

So I'm inclined to say that Baba's statements are true mysti-
cally, in a way that we can feel but can't see how to analyze. He
also stated that on occasion he was speaking his "own language."

I think his words, like religious beliefs, should be evaluated in
terms of their devotional efficacy rather than by trying to compare them to one's own worldview. I'd say Baba's influence is not
that of a gloriously spiritual person so much as that of the higher
from a particular angle of exposure.

He memorably stated, "I have come not to teach but to
awaken." That may say it all.

If you read about Meher Baba, in particular if you read several
books about him by the quite different persons, male and female,
who knew him well and whose solid character comes through in
the scrupulous candor of their writings, it dawns on you, "My
God, there really *are* people like this!"

Sheriar Press publishes books by and about Meher Baba. All
of them are of high literary quality, which also says something
about him. One I'd recommend to skeptics is He Gives the
Ocean (2006) by Najoo Savak Kotwal, about her years of experiences with Baba and his "mandali" or closest devotees. The genuineness of the love that's there can't be missed. If people can
sneer at this heartfelt and most comprehending book, at least
we'll know that it's no use to reason with them.

IX

Ramana Maharshi was, by the reckoning of many, the twentieth century's sage of sages, a spiritual knower and teacher of Himalayan stature. Following a death-like experience at the age of seventeen, he left everything behind and over time developed into a great yogi around whom a spiritual community grew up.

Like Meher Baba and allors generally, he lived without luxury or even much physical comfort. His renown reached the spiritually-minded in all parts of the world.

Again like Meher Baba, Ramana spent some of his early years in Samadhi (higher consciousness), unable to care for himself, before his "career" began in consequence of people's importunings. Dennett condemns as selfish those, such as contemplative monks, who devote their lives to "the purification of their souls," contrasting them with "hardworking nuns in schools and hospitals." (p.306) But there's good evidence that the best of humanity are impelled to turn inward, as a necessity and not as a choice, and that the outcome of their doing so is a level of service to the world that bustling activists can't match because it's free of egoism and informed by wisdom.

Why wouldn't scientists want to find out if that's so?

(I marvel how people are condemned as self-centered for taking something like the Silva course—for which see the chapter on imagination—that can do them some good and enable them to do others some good, whereas if they buy a sports car or a racing horse or they date someone glamorous, the same critics are full of praise for their knowledge of how to get the most out of life!)

Ramana revived and advocated an ancient practice called Self-enquiry, or *vichara marga*. It's an in-depth self-questioning with the words "Who am I?" Any thought that comes is hailed with the question who it is that thinks it. If there's boredom, pain, distraction, the question becomes for whom these things are. The purpose is to discover oneself as one truly is, as the all-inclusive reality or Self.

The following quotes are from Talks With Sri Ramana Maharshi, Vols. I to III (Sri Ramanasramam, Tiruvannamalai, South India, 1972). The book is mostly a record of Ramana's conversations with guests at the ashram, but there are a few revealing incidents in it, such as these:

"Somerset Maugham, a well-known English author, was on a visit to Sri Bhagavan [*I.e.* Ramana]. He also went to see Maj. Chadwick in his room and there he suddenly became unconscious. Maj. Chadwick requested Sri Bhagavan to see him. Sri Bhagavan went into the room, took a seat and gazed on Mr. Maugham. He regained his senses and saluted Sri Bhagavan. They remained silent and sat facing each other for nearly an hour. The author attempted to ask questions but did not speak. Maj. Chadwick encouraged him to ask. Sri Bhagavan said, 'All finished. Heart-talk is all talk. All talk must end in silence only.' They smiled and Sri Bhagavan left the room." (#550, p.517)

"When Sri Bhagavan was taking his bath a few *bhaktas* [devotees] were around him, speaking to themselves. Then they asked Him about the use of *ganja* (hashish). Sri Bhagavan had finished His bath by that time. He said 'Oh *ganja!* The users feel immensely happy when they are under its influence. How shall I describe their happiness! They simply shout *ananda!* [bliss] *ananda!* '... Saying so, He walked as if tipsy. The *bhaktas* laughed. He appeared as if He stumbled, placed His hands around 'A' and cried '*ananda! ananda!*'

"'A' records that his very being was transformed from that time." (#560, pp.519-20)

X

None of the allors I've mentioned opposed organized religion. All of them saw it as potentially helpful to a person's inner life. And all of them helped to lessen mutual antipathy among the religious, because whoever was a devotee of theirs knew better than to harbor hateful or prideful feelings. Sai Baba of Shirdi and Baba Lokenath, formidable figures now deceased for generations, notably had both Hindu and Muslim devotees in large numbers, and those devotees maintained harmony whether apart or in the closest company, as they do still.

And what of the allorists: the devotees who are most attuned to allors? I'll tell you what my experience has been. They're the opposite of brainwashed cultists—and much more alive, more individually distinctive, freer within themselves, more interesting, and more capable than most people are. Their compassion is strong but doesn't cramp the independence of others; it becomes tangible when appropriate and in ways that have fitting consequences.

They make opportunities available to the receptive and don't crowd them. Their sense of humor is always strong, a sign of mental health. Their thinking is the fruit of their own experiencing, not of indoctrination, and it doesn't bother them when people disagree with them. They're unlike fundamentalists and rationalists, who lean on ideologies and can't stand to be contradicted.

Genuine devotees aren't diminished by what doesn't affirm them. Their preference is not to control others but that others become more adept at controlling—and educating—themselves. Their faith is unconditional, so that nothing that happens threatens it. While morally demanding of themselves, they have flexibility in handling situations. They're further from hysteria than Freud himself was. They flow between life's rocks and don't beat themselves to bits on them.

There are of course secular-minded persons who'll refuse to consider whether higher humans exist. Healthy skepticism is one thing, denial another. It's scientific to want to be shown, unscientific to refuse to look.

In a world of such extremes and such variety—as in the historical juxtaposition of leaders like Hitler and Gandhi—the existence of lofty specimens of humanity may not be as improbable as doubters think. But, improbable or not, it's the case. If you question that, it'd be well to investigate or ask others to.

If you happen across saints, you'll find that it *feels* the most natural thing in the world. It's only when our thinking has been corralled by certain cultural constructs that we back off from the idea.

XI

What reasons are there for maintaining that the persons I've described in this chapter are genuine allors? I can think of several:

(a) Their words are never hackneyed, always fresh with direct perception. Pretenders can't duplicate that because they can't say what they really feel; they must imitate.

(b) They live in a way that very few could: without privacy and ever intruded upon by devotees and the anxious masses. They're not simply loving and giving, but ready to do whatever will most benefit someone at the moment. That could include anything from enabling persons to attain unimaginable states of consciousness to throwing rocks at them. They know what to do when. Their lives are conspicuously devoid of selfishness and self-centeredness. They might lose their temper—if that helps. Reputed allors who impose themselves on people sexually or who care about money or prestige or the roping in of recruits, on the other hand, are giving ample proof that they aren't real.

(c) It has often been said that you can tell saints by how you feel in their presence. The feeling is one of happiness and peace. This has nothing to do with what they're saying at the time or what the circumstances are. Visitors commonly arrive nervous and eager to get answers but go so quiet inside in an allor's presence as to forget what it was that they wanted to ask.

XII

When there are people in the world like the ones I've written of here, what does that say about religion, about humanity, about the nature of life?

And why are we listening to people like Harris and Hitchens and Dennett and Dawkins instead of to them?

And why aren't our scientists the ones asking these things?

It seems to me that if ever questions have deserved answering, these do. When will that start?

Six

Life after Death

I

Years ago something wild happened when I visited my friends the Glaziers. She had recently lost her brother and her father, both known for their humor and love of pranks. We had plans for the day, but there was a hiatus after breakfast while she attended to some housework and he to some academic work. I was looking over the books on their shelves upstairs and I asked her whether they had the Bhagavad Gita? She said it was there somewhere, but she wasn't able to turn it up. Perhaps a half hour later their little girl, then two or three, handed her mother a book and announced, "Bible." The book looked nothing like a Bible. It was a thin paperback with bright colors on its cover. It was the Bhagavad Gita.

Now, I can't say for sure *how* that happened. But one idea comes to mind pretty insistently.

All the major religions say we live on after our deaths, but they differ as to the details. Proof of survival couldn't clinch the over-all rightness of any religion, but it'd mean they're all more right than rationalists are in this area.

I've long thought that asking "What happens after we die?" may be equivalent to asking "What happens after we're born?" What doesn't? There's no reason it should be simple or uniform.

Is there good evidence that we continue in consciousness after the deaths of bodies? Yes, there's an abundance of it, and more all the time.

This doesn't mean we know beyond doubt. It means we should find out more.

Let's think about reincarnation. For years possible instances of it have been investigated. Ian Stevenson (1918-2007), a psychiatrist, was their premier investigator. His wife, a skeptic about reincarnation, gave him both encouragement and helpful criticism. He became a world traveler to meticulously study cases in which young children appear to have spontaneously recalled previous lifetimes.

Some of these children's accounts were detailed and capable of confirmation. When they were taken to villages and towns they had mentioned, where they had never been since birth, they knew their way around and accurately identified by name those they said were formerly their spouses, siblings, friends, and offspring. Incidents they described were also confirmed by those persons. Stevenson, ever careful and professional, labeled these cases "suggestive of" reincarnation.

When such things happen, with fraud and error not plausible as explanations, it's difficult to dismiss them.

Harris' book alludes to reincarnation noncommittally in passing, while the other three don't mention it. How rational can that be for those who'd size up the what and the how of ourselves?

Far more research into possible reincarnation should be taking place than is—should have been taking place right along. Western culture, both secular and religious, tends to have little liking for the idea of reincarnation, which goes against both the Christian and the rationalist worldviews. That fact is no doubt responsible for the general lack of attention to it. But how can true scientists participate in that unreadiness to know?

Lately rationalistic scientists have been trying to discredit out-of-body experiences by experimentally tricking the brain into believing that it's disembodied or occupying a separate body. Until they're ready to impartially investigate the *voluminous* reports about brain-dead patients who should theoretically perceive nothing but who upon awakening correctly recount what went on during the attempts to revive them, who describe veridically things they believe they saw from the ceiling and couldn't have seen from their beds even if they had been conscious then, who accurately detail goings-on in the hallway and conversations held out of the patient's earshot and even things that happened farther off—until those scientists take on such challenges, they're wasting their time and ours, feeding us pabulum and reinforcing instead of questioning their own prejudices.

II

Then there's the matter of ghosts. Unfortunately because of current assumptions, that expression—"ghosts"—has come to seem a bit comical and so makes the topic easy to laugh at. Even people who are satisfied that they've encountered such beings feel silly saying they "believe in ghosts." In the interest of fair evaluation, I'm proposing that we use another term, one that's not invidious.

"Discarnates" might do. But is it accurate? It says that these beings have no bodies. Yet reportedly they're seen, and sometimes felt and heard, to have solid bodies like our own. "Revenants" might do. But is it accurate? It says they've come again. But it seems at least as likely that they never left. "Spirits" might do. But it's redolent of religion, which only confounds matters.

I'm going to propose the term *ongoers*.

Such persons are perceived to have gone past the birth-life-time-death cycle without ceasing to be. They're no longer living humans (or animals) in our world, but they put in appearances within it, or so it's claimed by many.

There's an enormous literature on ongoers, containing incidents beyond the numbering. There are many reports from solid present-day witnesses, including trained observers such as police and firefighters. Over the past century and a half, hundreds if not thousands of cases have been recorded, many with fidelity and thoroughness. Alleged hauntings have been investigated in recent decades with the use of increasingly sophisticated equipment, taking them beyond the realm of rumor and legend.

I'd expect rationalists to say that the dead *can't* be conscious because their brains are decayed. (Lenin made that argument in Materialism and Empiriocriticism.) I guess there are two answers to that. One is that mind alone may be enough for consciousness, without brain being a factor. The other is that ongoers also have brains, only ones that, like the rest of their bodies, are of finer stuff than matter as we think of it.

In some places, such as Philadelphia, Pennsylvania, it's illegal to sell a haunted house without alerting the buyers in advance to its hauntedness. If there's no such thing as a haunting, it's strange to find that requirement in the law of a modern metropolis. Official note must've been taken of instances that reasonable people found to be indicative of it.

Dawkins discusses having mistakenly "seen" a malevolent spirit and "heard" an ongoer, both times with a natural explanation, implying that all hauntings are attributable to human error: "Constructing models is something the human brain is very good at. When we are asleep it is called dreaming; when we are awake we call it imagination or, when it is exceptionally vivid, hallucination...If we are gullible, we don't recognize hallucination or lucid dreaming for what it is and we claim to have seen or heard a ghost..." (p.91)

Is it hallucination when someone alone at home repeatedly sees a figure who, it's later learned, looks compellingly like photographic images of a departed tenant of that place? Is it hallucination when several persons feel a marked drop in temperature in a room in which unaccountable things have gone on? Is it hallucination when the electrical equipment of paranormal investigators detects something anomalous in a reputed "hot spot"? There are so many such happenings, and to glibly attribute them to human suggestibility reveals either a lack of familiarity with them or an ideologically-motivated attempt at an end-run around reality. Either way, it's intellectually sloppy at best.

I'll present here some disclosures of what seem to me to believably be encounters with ongoers. I don't say you should be a believer. I say what I've been saying all along: *that we should find out.*

Following are quotes from two e-mails I received in 2004 from a woman I've known for years. She's a professional person who has integrity and good sense and little or no interest in the paranormal. (I cited her e-mails in the second chapter during a discussion of whether evidence for the paranormal should be treated with respect.)

In the first e-mail she describes several things that had happened shortly after she and her boyfriend moved into an old house. The second e-mail contains the final item, a newer development. First:

"Was trying to sleep, looking out the bedroom window when I saw a shadow pass across the floor. It came from the middle of the floor and passed the floor in front of me, then the wall where the window is located. Nothing else happened that night."

"For the first couple of weeks, [one of her dogs] would growl at what appeared to be thin air. No noises, no sights or smells. He would just suddenly tense up and start growling softly. Over time, his growls lessened...but he is still often on alert and is very protective of me whenever I'm alone in the house."

"Was cleaning up in the kitchen and about to go upstairs when I saw a man out of the corner of my eye. He was in the entrance to the kitchen, and at first I thought someone was at the door. When I took a second look to see who was there, the figure was gone and there were no footprints or other indication that someone had been there. At the time I didn't have any real sense of who the person was other than that he was wearing a hat, but when my friend Liz asked me what he looked like, I instantly replied that he was middle-aged, wearing a hat and overcoat/raincoat. I don't know where that decision on age came from, it just came."

"Was taking a shower in the morning. I put my shampoo bottle (rectangular-bottomed, very stable) down in its usual spot on the shelf in the tub (also very flat and secure). About 1 minute later, the bottle suddenly rocked back and forth once before settling back down. Nothing else happened, although I did feel a draft in the bathroom, but attributed it to air coming through the vent in the ceiling."

"Around 9:30 p.m., heard what sounded like flute music coming from the den. It was playing a pretty melody. When you walked into the den, it stopped. If you hovered in the kitchen and listened for a few minutes, it would start again. [Her boyfriend] also heard it (after I convinced him to listen!), and had to admit that it definitely sounded like someone playing the flute."

"Another night a few days later, [her boyfriend] again heard the music at night (I wasn't home that night)."

"11:15 p.m.—Was running up the stairs to let the dogs out... As I almost topped the stairs, I saw to my left, out of the corner of my eye, a very bright streak of light. It was headed toward the back of the house ([her boyfriend's] office) from about the mid-section of the staircase railing at the top of the stairs. It was about knee-to-waist-height off the floor....It reminded me of a cat that had been spooked and was hightailing it out of the room..."

"11:45 p.m.—As I told [her boyfriend] what I saw (the light), I ended my remarks with the statement, 'That's the first time I've ever seen light.' Meaning, the first time I had seen light as a 'presence'....As soon as I finished saying the word 'light,' the [electric] candle in [his] window went on. It startled me so much that my heart skipped a few beats. His candle was the only one that wasn't on. The candles (7 total) are supposed to go on via timers at around 7 p.m.....The perfect timing of its popping on, just as I finished my thought out loud, was eerie. Too coincidental. Plus, the candle was directly where the light was headed (it's at the end of the hall, where I saw the light streak through.)"

"Was playing the piano, Debussy's Prelude La Fille aux Cheveux de Lin, when I 'heard' someone humming along with me (heard it with my right ear, as if someone were standing behind me, to my right shoulder, and humming along). It felt so natural, that I didn't stop playing or even get spooked....It could have been a deep-voiced woman or a man."

"Since December, I've sometimes felt a breeze of cool air across my right cheek when I'm in bed at night. Like a draft, except it never happens on the left side of my face, and [her boyfriend] never feels it."

"[Another of her dogs] kept disappearing all day. When it was dinnertime and she didn't appear, I went in search of her. Normally, she hangs out upstairs, particularly in the bedrooms. When she's downstairs, she'll stay in the dining room, but only if I'm downstairs as well. Tonight, I found her in the living room. What was strange was that she was sitting right next to the left arm (if you're sitting on it) of a chair....Her position was such that if someone were sitting in the chair, with their arm casually draped down, they would be petting her head. In fact, that's the first thing I thought of when I saw her. What was even stranger (I've known her behavior for almost 10 years now) is that when she saw me, instead of coming to me as she always does, she stayed there, sitting and wagging her tail in apology. I had to go up to her and talk to her, and even then she was reluctant to move. I told her that it was okay if she wanted to befriend this 'presence' in the house, but that I wanted her to be careful since I didn't know if the presence was friendly. She seemed to understand what I said, and looked up at the chair a couple of times while I was talking to her. When I asked her again to come to her dinner, she slowly followed me, looking back at the chair as she did so."

Lastly: "I have some exciting news to share. I now know at least one of my spirits. Before I fell asleep last night, I asked the spirit which I felt in the form of a breeze on my face....to show itself in my dream, if possible. Well, in my dream last night (one of those where you know you're dreaming and you control the dream as if you were awake, and you're very cognizant of it when you wake up as well [*I.e.* a lucid dream], the little boy showed himself. I was crouching in the middle of the bedroom, looking at my reflection in the window, when I saw the little boy right next to me, crouched identically to me, in the reflection. I guessed him to be about 5 years old. He had sandy-brown hair, with longish bangs. Slim, and he seemed a bit sad. He didn't look at me or the reflection in the window, rather he looked down at the floor. It was so real, I still feel it was an actual happening rather than within my dream. I'm sure he is the one who strokes my face with the cool breeze at night, in a comforting way. He may also be the one who streaked down the hall that one night, startled by my abrupt presence."

Not a great deal more happened before my friend moved on to a new home and a new job.

I wonder how Dawkins would analyze those experiences? For example, were my friend and her boyfriend jointly hallucinating when they repeatedly heard flute music that stopped as they approached its source? Was her one dog hallucinating when he kept growling at something they couldn't see? Was her other dog hallucinating when she behaved as though someone was sitting in a chair and stroking her head? And what would account for such *unusual* hallucinations, befalling both animals and humans?

III

One day maybe fifteen years ago I arrived at work amidst novel goings-on. Two of the custodians had played a prank on a third one, as a result of his having told them that he had just seen an ongoer.

As he recounted it, he had stepped out in front of the building to have a smoke. There are twin buildings on either side of the one he had come out of. They have front doors that are directly opposite one another, approximately 70 feet from where he stood. A young woman walked out of the front door of the building on his right and proceeded toward the front door of the other. The lower half of her body was transparent and became invisible nearer to the ground. She vanished before she reached the other door. He had hollered for his fellow custodians to come look, but they got there too late. He had her in view for, I'd guess, ten or twelve seconds—long enough to be sure about the characteristics of what he was viewing.

A fourth custodian, a young man whom I sized up as a rather

innocent person, solemnly informed me that morning that when he was a little boy he had a vivid dream in which he was with a very loving elderly couple in their home. When he gave his parents a complete account of the dream, they told him he had described his late grandparents, whom he had never known, and their house. He wasn't one of those mocking his co-worker.

These things happen. They happen again and again and again and again and again and again and again. Why would we make assumptions about them, either pro or con, and not do our best to establish what they're really about?

IV

Several years ago my longest-term friend, a lifelong atheist and a disbeliever in any sort of afterlife, had to change his mind about the latter. He taped and mailed to me several of medium John Edward's television broadcasts. Watching the shows had convinced him that we do indeed outlive our lifetimes. Let me add that he wasn't pleased, as he had no desire for an afterlife. Nor has he taken an interest in that prospect in the meantime; this wasn't wishful thinking on his part.

Professional skeptics have said they could duplicate what John Edward does. I don't see them doing it, however. And I'm afraid I can't see how they could. When you face several dozen strangers, offer something precise about a deceased person that one of them picks up on, and then give details or anecdotes or private jokes that the person affirms as correct, what you're doing can't be faked. And the details are scarcely generic. "Smelly feet" is one that I recall from the tapes. After-the-fact interviews with some of these people make it clear just how accurate Edward was.

Are the program's staffers making Edward look better by editing out his goofs? If so, it may not matter as long as they don't edit anything *in*. I haven't read about any audience member crying foul. If Edward isn't in contact with the dead, I think we're owed an explanation of how he gets his results.

So new interviewing, theorizing, and experimenting are in order.

V

On November 4, 1995 I had a reading from an upstate New York psychic named Laura Mainville. Laura is a longtime professional psychic and was in her middle fifties at the time. She's a stout, comfortable, religious and good-natured woman who had earlier had a local television program in which people called in questions and she gave psychic answers. A quite honest woman I know had served as her sidekick on the show.

I went to Laura because I was searching for work after being laid off and was ready to leave Ithaca, where I had lived for decades, for someplace new. Her disclosures turned out not to be pertinent to my job search, but on other things she was often resoundingly accurate, including giving spot-on thumbnail descriptions of people whom I knew and she didn't.

She could be very right and very wrong, I found. Over a number of readings, it became clear to me that she knew *me* through and through, including idiosyncratic particulars she couldn't have picked up by observation.

I should add here that neither Laura nor I owes the other anything and that I have no ulterior motive for giving her publicity (which I don't think she needs anyway) and do so strictly for the sake of this book after getting her permission to.

She always taped the readings for me, so what follows is a transcript of parts of that '95 reading, with commentary by me in brackets:

> LM: And in sharing this with you, somehow we're touching with spirit world. Many years ago there was a lady that lived up on, I believe, Hector Street....And her name was Mrs. Tiffany. Very lovely lady, rather slender built. Kind of regal; she really took care of herself. And she was in her late eighties when I met her. [I was puzzled as to where she could be going with this, as I imagine you

are.] But I feel like you have somebody like that in spirit. That cared for books [notice that point], that cared for herself. I can't say she was prim and proper, but she was regal when she walked across a room. She reminds me so much of Mrs. Tiffany.

JG: How old is she?

LM: This lady in spirit is probably—When she went into spirit she was 65, 67.

JG: Okay, we're talking about books. I had a boss at one time at a library at the University of Pennsylvania whose name was Martha Lightwood. She died a few years ago. She was around that age, I think. [According to the Social Security Death Index she was 68.]

LM: Give or take a little. She comes close to you in spirit.

JG: We were friends. We got along well.

LM: Not pushy-type. Or not, you know, in too tight. It's just her presence is here. And she just reminded me so much of this lady...

JG: It might be she, but I can't be sure...Regal? It's hard to be sure on that.

LM: A stately lady that knew how to walk and carry herself.

JG: Maybe. Yeah, maybe.

LM: She said, "I'm just here for a quick reference." That's all she's sayin'.

JG: Quick reference! Okay she was the head of reference at—[Stacks work is usually under the head of circulation, not of reference.]

LM: Okay, that was just an identifier so you'd know

you had the right person. God bless her and she's welcome.

"Takes care of books" and "takes care of herself" are so. "Regal" is a judgment call, but Mrs. Lightwood, or Marty, always dressed well, wore high heels, and had an air of easy authority. She was good-humored and witty, so the "quick reference" remark was convincingly in character for her. Laura had unexpectedly given me something evidential at the very outset, something that no "cold reading" could have approximated to.

Further along in the reading came this:

LM: "You're not to worry; there's a place for you." That's what I'm hearing. Ah, grandfather in spirit? Shorter than you? [I knew only my maternal grandfather, who was shorter than I am.] Kind of—I don't know, one shoulder seems, there's something with this one shoulder. [My grandfather in his later years had one shoulder that was noticeably higher than the other.] You're not a physical person but he was quite physical. [Correct. I like to walk but have never especially enjoyed garden work or repairing things or the like; my grandfather was always busy with them.]

JG: Yeah.

LM: Very quick, very sharp, words came out of his mouth; he had the answers. [Correct.] He says "I'm here to help you." (Chuckles) "I'm here to help," and that isn't the way he says it, he says [aggressively] "I'm here to help!" [Yes, if anything had to be done or any question was undecided, Grand-dad went into his take-charge mode and sounded like that.] And I think he will do that. Ah, would there be a reason for his spirit to be up around Vermont for a while?

JG: No, I don't think he was ever there in his life.

LM: Okay, there's something in Vermont, either

somebody he knows or something. And he says when he gets done up there then he'll be down here.

JG: H'm!

Later, when I was out in the parking lot waiting for the cab to take me from Freeville back to Ithaca, I remembered that a young cousin of mine, whom my grandfather had known as a small child, had moved to Vermont not long before and was about to be married but hadn't yet found employment. So he also could've used some help, making my grandfather's Vermont connection a "hit" after all.

I think anyone who visited a psychic and was given the kinds of revelations I was would find it hard to accept the rationalist version of the world. I've also been to ineffective psychics and fraudulent ones and dubious mediums, so I'd ask people to be careful and critical-minded in seeking out a medium or a psychic and not to make too much of even a string of bad readings.

VI

Somewhat over a decade ago I had a series of dreams in which I came face to face with my great aunt, who several years before had died of cancer in her early eighties. It may be to the point that the last time I saw her was in her final days after she had moved into a care facility. As I was about to leave with my mother (who lived in Eastern Pennsylvania, as she did, while I was going to return to upstate New York), Aunt Peg said, "I'll never see him again" and began crying. The old woman she shared the room with snapped something like, "Don't be such a baby! You'll see him in heaven."

There were four or five of these dreams. I wish I had written all of them down, but I remember the features of some of them pretty well. Each began as the usual, unremarkable kind of dream. Then it's as though that dream got hijacked and made to serve a purpose.

In the first one, I was standing in the darkened dining room of a house that looked like that of another aunt of mine, and

I felt as if I shouldn't be there. The kitchen door opened and someone started through—someone ancient and feeble. At first I thought it might be my Aunt Lid, Aunt Peg's sister; but then I realized who it was. There followed a back-and-forth between my thinking that it couldn't be she, because she was dead, and my seeing quite well that it *was* she. After a little of that I woke up in agitation.

In the dreams that followed the circumstances were different, but in each of them the situation resolved itself suddenly into an encounter with my aunt. And each time I reacted in the same way—shocked incredulity, certainty that it was so, more incredulity, then awakening.

In one dream I seemed to be about fourteen years old and I was riding with my father into the apron of our driveway. We got out, and I glanced toward the kitchen window. In one half of it my mother (then living) was looking out. In the other half was Aunt Peg, regarding me and weeping, I took it from happiness. Again there was the ping-ponging of shakenness and conviction before I awoke.

In waking life I surely would've thought that I could be seeing an ongoer, removing the feeling of impossibility that was the source of my turmoil. But in the dreams that thought didn't occur to me; perhaps it was blocked.

Much later, during a reading, Laura Mainville announced that someone was there. Laura asked, "Who are you?" The answer she heard was, "I'm the maiden aunt." Laura didn't know that I had had an unmarried aunt, let alone that Aunt Peg had teasingly insisted on referring to herself by that title over the years. The term "maiden aunt" is so old-fashioned and unused as to be a fine identifier, I think.

I had another significant dream not too long ago. As background to it, I'll explain that I had been praying weekly for a handful of ancestors whom I remember or know of, offering prayers in an attempt to assist them in their heightening. When it came to my mother's brother, my Uncle Bob, I included him after the others; he had sometimes been ill-humored toward me and I wasn't eager to concentrate on him. The night of the first day I prayed for him, the memorable dream arrived.

In it, I was in a desert and was visiting the small home of an elderly, motherly woman with whom I felt very much at ease. I never got a look at this woman during the dream, even when she was present and there was no apparent reason I couldn't; her identity was a mystery to me.

Also present was a man I knew to be "an uncle." This man didn't look particularly like Uncle Bob but was about the same size and build (short, slight). He smoked cigarettes, as my uncle had, but *his* smoke was white rather than gray and I knew it to be clean and harmless. He wore a white T-shirt, which might've been meant to signify benignity also.

At one juncture I was outside the house while the uncle and the woman were sitting on the porch. I was looking through some magazines that had belonged to my grandfather. The uncle told me that I was welcome to borrow anything that I fancied.

I woke up finding the dream very interesting. Before I had time to analyze it, I asked myself who the woman I was visiting could've been? A phrase came into my head: "A grandmother who isn't visited by her grandchildren."

My maternal grandmother, who was Uncle Bob's mother, died of Alzheimer's disease after several years in a nursing home. I went to see her there only one time because she was so obviously unaware of what was taking place around her that there was no reason to go again. She sat in a chair with her eyes closed, repeating "see—see --see," apparently obsessed with sight: I'm sure her glaucoma medication had been discontinued to save money, as there was no chance of her condition improving. I don't think her other two grandchildren went there many times, either, for the same reason.

So she *was* a grandmother who wasn't visited by her grandchildren. I'd never have guessed that she had known what was going on in that room, but maybe she had from an out-of-body perspective; or maybe she found out after dying.

Apparently she was hurt to think that we had given up on

her. Yet her presence in the dream was mellow and affectionate, with no hint of anger or distancing.

Why was she in a desert in the dream? I figure it for a pun—because she felt deserted.

The next five or six times that I prayed for Uncle Bob, I got a feeling of happiness from his picture. He wasn't very happy in the latter part of his life, so I think it was his way of telling me that he's doing well now. And I pray each time that he'll always hereafter be happy, whatever may befall him.

If that dream was my subconscious at work, I confess that I don't see what it was aiming to do.

VII

When Ignaz Semmelweis said that women could escape puerperal fever if physicians would wash their hands after assisting one in childbirth and before assisting the next, he was attacked by the medical establishment of his time just as rabidly as Dawkins attacks believers in "the supernatural" today. What Semmelweis was saying invoked invisible agency (we call the agents "microbes") and therefore went against the scientific paradigm of his day. The establishment "knew better." But Semmelweis was right, as Pasteur subsequently explained with his germ theory of disease.

Dismissing evidence because it goes against a paradigm makes for a sorry kind of science. With that in mind, I conclude with this

OPEN LETTER TO RICHARD DAWKINS:

Sir,

By attempting to explain away ongoers in terms of some people's mistaken perceptions and gullibility, you've pandered to prejudice and flattered self-satisfied ignorance, mental laziness, and incuriousness.

By offering an anecdote as your refutation of the reality of life after death, you've disrespected the disciplined application, the unbending impartiality, and the unremitting honesty of true science.

Do you think Charles Darwin, who didn't let the Christian beliefs he started with prevent him from being faithful to the facts he uncovered, would be proud of you for sloughing off all of the relevant evidence?

Your cavalier treatment of this issue constitutes scientific malpractice and—because rationalism would be refuted by proof that we survive bodily death—what the uncharitable might call moral cowardice.

To avoid these imputations, you can put your views at honorable risk. That is, you can review paranormal data as you would biological data and confer with seasoned field investigators and with reputable witnesses to the phenomena. Then you an tell us frankly what you've learned and what you think as a result, and why.

If you refuse to do that yet go on saying there's no survival, you'll be right at least about that of your credibility.

-John Gibson

SEVEN

CONTRA SPONG

I

Scientists no longer wear religions' doctrines as blinders. Now we have religionists who wear the "scientific" doctrines of rationalism as blinders. Foremost among them is theologian John Shelby Spong, who has thereby won himself a loyal following and a great deal of controversy.

The retired Episcopal bishop would be a new Luther and so has titled his autobiography <u>Here</u> <u>I</u> <u>Stand</u>. He wants a second Reformation, arguing that traditional Christianity has been refuted by advances in scientific knowledge and must adapt or perish.

He thinks religion can be saved if certain beliefs are abolished: those favorable to theism, to miracles, and to "the supernatural." He'd eliminate God as personal and active, prayer, angels, demons, virgin birth, and physical resurrection. His rationale is that no self-honest person of today can credit such phenomena.

Spong would retain God as Ground of All Being, religious congregations, and Jesus as exemplifying the divine within the human, not as a Godman. He favors religion, it appears, as instrumental for the recruiting and organizing of people for social activism, and for its liturgical ability to make them feel better about themselves.

He's dedicated to inclusiveness, having worked for civil rights, and is presently working for the rights of sexual minorities. For him the church is more a rallying point for social justice than a means of assistance to individual spiritual development. (It could, of course, be fully both.)

In view of the rest of what he says, we might wonder if the belief that he professes in some sort of an afterlife is thrown in to humor us lest he push us too far at once? He says next to nothing about why he believes in it or what it might be like. Why would he think it exists?

He presents himself as more representative than original, and it's true that views increasingly approximating to his have been prevalent for generations in the more progressive Protestant seminaries. Theologians like Dietrich Bonhoeffer, Paul Tillich, and Bishop John A. T. Robinson are precursors in his intellectual line, and he advances the main thrust of their thinking. So it may be that the additional modernizing of religion, if it occurs, will pass through and not around his position.

That's why what he says deserves analysis. Theology matters, when it does, because it can (mis)guide.

II

Spong cites the use of coffee, tobacco, alcohol, and recreational drugs, as well as the incidence of depression, suicide, genocide, racism, and other such societal afflictions as reflecting the death of belief in the theistic God.

He traces religion to a point in our evolution where, according to him, the realization that each of us must die threatened to paralyze us with anxiety. "An emotional thermostat designed to control that hysteria had to be created," he alleges, because "survival *required* it. The creation of the various theistic religious forms was a major component—indeed *the* major component—of that thermostat. (John Shelby Spong, A New Christianity For A New World, HarperSanFrancisco, 2001, p.43) And now that theistic belief is waning, he says, these addictions and untoward behaviors are returning to the world in force, just as might've been predicted.

But there's no evidence that humanity was ever actually or potentially threatened by traumatic mental paralysis. Had there been such a problem, natural selection wouldn't have solved it with something as elaborate as theistic religion, when all that would've been necessary is the survival of the kind of human who doesn't dwell on the inevitability of death. Look around you at disbelievers in an afterlife. Are they stricken, helpless, given to extremes of behavior?

What of genocide? Well, it has been with us since long before the religious decline of recent centuries. We're told that the theistic ancient Hebrews, for example, committed genocide against the inhabitants of the land of Canaan. The Medieval leadership of the Catholic church, which was quite theistic, ordered genocide against the Cathar population in France. If we say that people commit genocide because they're no longer theists *and* because they *are* theists, have we really accounted for genocide?

Coffee was brought to us by theistic Arabs centuries ago, and they were addicted to it before we were. As for racism: American's slave owners, three centuries of them, were among the most Bible-quoting and churchgoing folk in the land.

Drug use, suicide, depression, and the like seem to be related to the widespread conviction that life is without meaning. That connects to the fading of religious commitment in general. If people no longer want theism *but* still want to be religious, as Spong postulates, wouldn't you expect a nearly universal upsurge in the popularity of Buddhism and other non-theistic forms of religion? Where is it?

I suspect that our hedonistic culture and our lengthy life expectancy have seduced many of us away from religion and that it's mainly when something hurtful happens that we go back. We see regularly that people in trouble pray. The 90% of us in the United States who say we believe in God are theists, even if hibernating ones.

I don't find critical thinking in what the bishop says. He likes an idea and comes up with thoughts that support it, but he doesn't ask himself what's against it, what could invalidate it. For that reason he isn't difficult to answer.

He doesn't mention a rival theory of the origin of theistic

religion. Hindus and the late Christian mystic and scholar Rudolf Steiner are among those who've said that in former times
we were more open than now to spiritual influences and higher
beings, and that having lost that openness we compensate with
intellectuality. Could this be true? One reason to think it may be
is that people today do seem less spiritually adept in general than
were people of the past. Consider that the great scriptures were
written and the great religions founded long ago, the most recent
of them a millennium and a half before our time.

The bishop is given to referring to the founders and earlier
practitioners of those religions as "our primitive ancestors" (A
New Christianity For A New World, p.55), as though persons
unacquainted with Freud, Darwin, and sociology must be inferior
to ourselves in spirituality. "Our primitive ancestors" somehow
managed to bequeath to us extraordinary faiths—profoundly
motivating, emotionally compelling, intuitively right, beautiful
in their expression far beyond what recent people have been able
to utter. Today several billion humans continue to practice those
faiths, many of us being notably bettered by doing so. Consider-
ing that those long-ago humans did something monumental and
divinely revealing that we don't know how to replicate, who is it
that's deserving of being termed primitive?

III

"(N)o definition of God is to be equated with God," writes
Spong (A New Christianity For A New World, p. 83) "The God
beyond theism cannot be bound by human creeds." (p.137) "We
have acted time after time as if the God we have experienced
could be or has been captured in and bound by the words of our
scriptures, our creeds, and our doctrines." (p.237) "There is no
way that we can say that God *is* anything." (p.237) "We have pretended that we can actually say 'God is ——,' arrogantly filling in
the blanks with our concepts." (p.238) While I'm inclined to like
those remarks, I have to wonder how it is that he doesn't recognize them as applying to his own attempt to define God out of
consciousness, will, and the capacity for decision and action?

My view is that we have to understand God through our involvement in the higher, not through speculatively granting *or* denying him attributes.

He refers above to "the God we have experienced." Is the kind of experiencing of God that he alludes to that of mystics? He doesn't specify. And how does he reconcile belief in some version of God—any version—with the heft of what he believes, which is rationalism?

Spong: "...I do not define God as a supernatural being. I do not believe in a deity who can help a nation win a war, intervene to cure a loved one's sickness, allow a particular athletic team to defeat its opponent, or affect the weather for anyone's benefit. I do not think that it is appropriate for me to pretend that those things are possible when everything I know about the natural order of the world I inhabit proclaims that they are not." (A New Christianity For A New World, pp.3-4) Wouldn't he have to know more about God, rather than only knowing things things about the world, to be able to say what he's saying? What he relies on isn't knowledge at all but the most prized concept of rationalism: impossibility.

Spong: "Increasingly human beings learned that their world operated according to fixed laws, which brooked no interference from any external source, divine or otherwise." (John Shelby Spong, Why Christianity Must Change or Die, HarperSanFrancisco, 1998, pp.34-35) Just how did human beings increasingly learn that? Would it even be possible to learn such a thing? It's a *supposition,* not a discovery!

Belief in the theistic God is dying or dead, he says, because science has been able to explain the occurring of natural phenomena. Previously, he suggests, we thought of them as God's doing; but now we know better. Well, some religious people always did and still do consider everyday health matters, victory or defeat in war, and life's other routine events as resulting from divine action. In fact, most theists will say that whatever happens is "God's will." But it's only the rare event, one said to violate "the laws of nature," that was and is taken to be *miraculous.*

As for whether miracles exist, he'd have to investigate. He can't rationally pronounce against it *ex cathedra*, bishop or no.

The idea of a divine healing "that is the result of human petition for intercession turns God into a being who does our will." (A New Christianity For A New World, pp.195-6) There's a distinction to be made here. If God or some higher being were to indiscriminately do as we asked every time we made a request, (s)he'd both be an instrument of our will and do many things that are bad for us. But those objections needn't apply if such a being were to *choose on some occasions,* for good reasons, to do something we appealed for. If you're a child and your father at times does something you ask him to do, does that reduce him to a discretionless stooge of yours?

IV

Faith, which Spong plainly sees as unrealistic, would be the most consequential victim of his intended reformation. He charges that faith produces "an immature person who needs to be taken care of by the supernatural deity," which is "for me nothing more than a delusion designed to keep human beings dependent and childlike." He exults in the insecurity of being without that. (A New Christianity For A New World, p.xxi)

But, honestly, who wants to be insecure in a treacherous world? If he thinks God can do nothing for us, why not admit that that's a tragedy? What's the virtue of this sour-grapes view that we're better off facing life's trials and terrors on our own? (When someone doesn't show up to plow the bishop's driveway, does he say, "Good! Good! Adversity! Builds character!"? Or does he say something less polite?)

He announces, "We know that the theological perspective, suggesting that our frail humanity is always in need of a divine protector, does not work. It presents us with a deity that we must please, placate, flatter, and beg, one whose power is so overwhelming that we are reduced to a childlike dependency." (A New Christianity For A New World, pp.194-5) The dependency is there, even if he insists the help isn't.

I've found, as have people throughout the ages, that to praise a deity during worship and mean it, and to correspondingly lower oneself, is to grow in devotion, which is of the truest benefit and brings deliverance from minds mired in dissatisfaction and pessimism. The earlier style of praising and self-abasing may strike us as humorous, but the practice is legitimate. If he doesn't know this, it's because his tradition has grown decadent and so has (a) forgotten why it formerly did such things, and (b) done them, if at all, only ritualistically and without attendant comprehension, feeling, and energy.

He doesn't realize that we're talking not about a way of relating to a being who could equally well not exist, but about what our own nature must undergo to be fulfilled: the surrender of its lower to its higher tendencies.

Ask a Muslim who revels in being a "slave of Allah" what that feels like. You'll hear, I think, that it's worth-enhancing and beautiful—the opposite of what one might be wont to conjecture.

The higher is freedom, not oppression. Acknowledging our dependence on the higher adds to our boldness and capability; it doesn't detract from them. In Hinduism the ideal devotee is Hanuman, who excels in resourcefulness, might, and bravery. The goal is to be like him while asking the help of the higher: not to bemoan one's weakness but to trust in God while doing as one can.

Bowing ourselves lessens our vanity and our inner commitment to remaining consistent with our less-than-splendid pasts. Spong treats it as though it were detrimental to our self-respect. So conceived, self-respect would be pridefulness. True self-respect goes nicely with admitting error, asking forgiveness, and requesting help.

The bishop repeatedly complains of an attempt to make us into dependent children. Having faith and being childlike are surely what Christianity, his own religion, is about. What did Jesus extol, demand, condemn the lack of, so much as faith, according to the Christian scriptures? And what did he call for, according to them, as irreplaceable for entering the kingdom of God, if not becoming childlike?

Spong says he calls Jesus Lord, but he despises Jesus' thinking as it has come down to us. He must believe either that Jesus actually agreed with him despite what's written, a thesis for which there's no evidence, or that Jesus understood less about God and faith than Spong does. Why call someone Lord if you're smarter than he is?

(Maybe it's time for Spongians to leave Jesus behind, having outgrown him, and adopt a substitute messiah? No less an authority than Jean-Paul Sartre has said that Che Guevara was the most perfect man of our time. Or why not choose Spong himself? Only that could assure that he and his lord would agree completely.)

To be childlike isn't to be childish or incapable. It's to live from our innocence and lovingness and to trust unconditionally. One who does that can handle the greatest of responsibilities without being crushed by them or by such guilt as attends failure in them or by suffering caused to others in the performance of them. Many who've devoted their lives to the higher and to heightening say that not passivity and immaturity but strength and sensitivity are derived from being childlike.

Not only Jesus but allors throughout history have said the same thing. We've no record of any of them having contradicted it. And they've spoken from their personal recognition, without reference to one another. Countless everyday people have echoed their words from their own experiences. Remind me: who exactly is Bishop Spong that he needn't so much as consider what they've told us?

V

And what of prayer? The Dalai Lama, a professed atheist, regularly joins people in praying. There's no hypocrisy in this. He recognizes that there's efficacy in it whether there's a God or not. But Spong, who comes from a theistic tradition, decries prayer as a waste of time. He tells us how he prayed for years, woodenly, getting nothing out of it.

It seems he prayed on behalf of lists of people each time, making the process mechanical and tedious. He finally gave it up. Now, he says, "Prayer for me is *living*." (A New Christianity For A New World, p.198, italics in original) Prayer for most of us who pray is *praying*. What can he say to us who feel connection in prayer, who receive from it glimpses of something high and free and affirming of ourselves, who come away from it with minds at peace and a greater ability to go forward with courage? Is our testimony nothing? It's likely that he killed his capacity for prayer by regarding it as a chore. And no doubt he brought to it the earlier stages of the materialist views that he now espouses.

It's not as though no one knows anything about prayer. Everything from simple self-help books to lengthy scholarly tomes has been written on it. Any number of everyday people could give him pointers on how to do it. From my experiences and those of countless others, I think prayer makes a real difference within oneself over time if one does it in earnest and with a readiness to proceed where guided.

Praying means developing antennae to the higher. Yes, it's sometimes about requests and concerns, within a mandala that includes gratitude, reflectiveness, contentment, receptivity, awareness, and new mental grooves.

By dismissing prayer as worthless, Spong presents himself as *the* authority on it. And that on the basis of what? Of having done it badly and given up! Isn't that breathtaking?

VI

"In the Christian West today," writes Spong, "we are far too sophisticated to erect idols of wood or stone and call them our gods. We know that such an activity has no credibility." (A New Christianity For A New World, p.60) The point he's making is that Christians have defined God in terms of the doctrines of their religion, and that this is as much idolatry as is the constructing of physical idols. But what I want to go into here is what his example reveals about him.

He has just insulted some three quarters of a billion Hindus who worship God as gods present to us within idols. That's from someone who's libertarian in religious viewpoint and a fierce opponent of discrimination against any group!

Nevertheless, he also insults Buddhists. While he cites them approvingly because they "experience bliss or transcendence in meditation" without attributing "this to contact with the supernatural" (Why Christianity Must Change or Die, p.57), he ignores the fact that Buddhists have always reported that at a certain stage of their practice the ability to work miracles is attained; they refuse to work them, but they're clear that to work them is perfectly possible. Spong, who praises what they do when that suits his anti-theistic purpose, denies, as we've seen, that anything of a miraculous character can exist.

What the Buddhists are saying isn't myth, folklore, or doctrine; it's grounded in historical and contemporary experience. But he won't maintain an open mind as to it out of deference to them, despite his admiration for them. Why this unwillingness to let his opinions be challenged and informed by what others have found out?

Besides belittling Buddhists and Hindus, he insults all theists without exception, not by following another course than theirs but by representing them as immature, pre-scientific, and absolutely, unqualifiedly *wrong*. It's not a matter of "We worship this way and you worship that way" but of differences rendered irreconcilable by his own triumphalism. In this, too, he's in tune with the proudly-brandished intolerance of rationalists.

Spong has never thought of it this way, I'm sure, but what he's proposing is neo-fundamentalism. It's neo- because the dividing wedge is no longer the supposed total factual accuracy of the Bible but the naturalism that he has grafted onto those elements of Christianity that he'd keep. It leaves no room for disagreement. According to him it's a *fact* that there's nothing to theism, and a *fact* that there's no gain from praying, and a *fact* that lowering oneself before God depletes manliness. Contrary views aren't weighed.

No avowed exclusivist could do a more thorough job of arousing conflict over purportedly factual notions. Yet the things he regards as settled fact are unproved if not disproved (such as that the laws of nature are inviolable and that prayer does no good) when not unprovable (such as that God is the Ground of All Being). And *this* is the new, science-friendly Christianity?

It's not only the Christian tradition but all the rest as well that this second Luther has plans for. He proposes a kind of syncretism. He writes: "Having surrendered the security-producing tribal claims which suggest that our way is the only way [although he has suggested exactly that himself], we will be free to recognize that we do not have to say to another person that his or her way into the holy is wrong. Those who once called themselves Catholic and Protestant, orthodox and heretic, liberal and evangelical, Jew and Muslim, Buddhist and Hindu, will all find a place in the ecclesia [Spongian places of worship] of the future. There being and nonbeing, substance and shadow, can be accepted—no, even celebrated." (Why Christianity Must Change or Die, p.214)

I don't think most of us particularly wish to celebrate heresy, nonbeing, or shadow. When religion is about results and not about theories, there's no need for such zany accommodations.

Spong: "The ecclesia of the future will exhibit a renewed dedication to the search for truth. It will never claim that it already possesses truth by divine revelation. It will seek to enlighten people by honoring their questions. It will not seek to propagandize people by claiming that it has all the answers." (Why Christianity Must Change or Die, p.214) So the greatest of mystical insights, utterly crackpot figments, and meaningless theological slush, all are to be affirmed. Religion is to enjoy the hollowest of victories, becoming at once all-comprehensive and empty.

There's heightening to be attained through all of the great traditions for those who'll work and sacrifice to get it. The bishop would welcome all of these images of truth while dismissing each. Not unfair to any single one, he'd be unfair to every single one, embracing and nullifying them in the same motion. While he speaks of a search for religious truth, it's obvious that he doesn't believe there's any to be found. If he did, he'd look for it instead of engaging in this leveling that indiscriminately puts sense on a par with nonsense.

VII

The extraordinary can happen in religion. Bishop Spong's attitude—superior, scoffing, closed off—makes it improbable that around him anything extraordinary *will* happen. That's a shame.

By accommodating rationalism and abandoning infinintention he has made true religion less believable to his followers, and that's what his reformation boils down to. If religion isn't about heightening, it isn't really about anything.

Therefore I conclude this chapter with an

OPEN LETTER TO BISHOP
JOHN SHELBY SPONG:

Sir,

You're not wrong to oppose fundamentalism and to ally yourself with the rights and the opportunities of minorities, as religion should have no part in oppression and bigotry. Where you're wrong is in thinking that old religious beliefs and practices denote an understanding of the world that's primitive or pre-scientific. If you'll look upon them as loftlore, you'll find they haven't and can't become outdated.

In your writings I find only disillusionment with religion, disguised by bravado.

Religion deals with the outer world first through heightened receptiveness to the inner, part of which is accomplished through prayer. You'd reverse that, psyching people and devoting all their efforts to altering our environing circumstances. And your "realism" is based on the illusions of ideologues who say they speak for the sciences but won't let them do their work of finding out what the world is truly like.

The best thing you can do, I'm convinced, is to re-examine your accumulated and mutually supporting views about how things are. That doesn't mean yielding to fundamentalism. It means yielding to true religion.

If you acquaint yourself with people of love, allorance, and faith who have no axe to grind and for whom God isn't an abstraction; if you listen attentively to their experiences and observations instead of conferring with theologians and atheists; if you look at the evidence instead of flattering yourself that the world is simple and that you've mastered its nature; if you learn of and talk with allors, as you should long since have done; if you rediscover prayer as invaluable for heightening; if you abandon your know-it-all cynicism and realize that being innocent and childlike *is* the religious way: then what you say therafter will please the most heart-heeding religious people and not those who despise them and religion and, yes, you.

-John Gibson

EIGHT

ISLAMIA

I

Increasingly all Muslims are being made to pay for what a few Muslims are doing to others. I'm unwilling to see Muslims defamed or mistreated, either in person or in the pages of books. Those who do that in the name of reason only create moral confusion in themselves and their readers.

Harris: "To see the role that faith plays in propagating Muslim violence, we need only ask why so many Muslims are eager to turn themselves into bombs these days." (p.32) "So many Muslims"? They're the tiniest fraction of the global Muslim population. Shahla Ali, an assistant New York State attorney general, replied well to a similar remark (as reported in *India Abroad* for September 15, 2006, p.M2): "It is a religion of a billion plus people and if they all wanted to blow themselves up there would be nothing standing."

Harris's answer to the question he posed is: "(B)ecause the Koran makes this activity [suicide bombing] seem like a career opportunity." (p.32) As for the Koran or Qur'an, it doesn't commend suicide warfare and it expressly rejects compulsion in religion, the starting of wars, and the harming of the innocent. It's quintessentially rationalistic to pick out some verses and pretend the rest don't matter. They all matter, or else none of them does.

Has Harris ever paused to think that his overwhelming task of abolishing all religion might not be necessary if he explored what leads some to interpret their scriptures as incitements to malice and violence, *especially when so many other members of the same religion don't?*

Harris: "Subtract the Muslim belief in martyrdom and jihad, and the actions of suicide bombers become completely unintelligible....(I)nsert these peculiar beliefs, and one can only marvel that suicide bombing is not more widespread." (p.33) Dead wrong! For years secular revolutionaries of non-Muslim background have committed suicide bombings in Sri Lanka. In fact, they pioneered the technique. Rajiv Gandhi was killed in India along with a number of others by such a Sri Lankan bomber. Since non-religious motives are *sufficient* to explain suicide attacks by these secular bombers, we can't say even that a religious motive is *necessary,* let alone sufficient as Harris asserts, to explain suicide attacks by Muslim bombers. More investigation is apposite here!

What of his statement that it's a marvel suicide bombing isn't more widespread? Doesn't it tacitly acknowledge that such aggression is occasioned by circumstances? After all, Islam has been around for a millennium and a half; and, while there have been large and vivid exceptions, for most of that time there has been no conflict between it and the rest of the world. If the basic character of this religion is what assures that there'll be warfare, why has warfare been only intermittent while the worship and Qur'an-reading have been constant?

II

India Abroad for December 15, 2006 contains an interview with Akeel Bilgrami, an American secular philosopher who was raised in India as a Muslim. He states:

"I have no problem saying that Osama bin Laden is a monster and I do not hesitate to say that the jihadists who have used terrorism should not be condoned. But I also say that it is... morally moronic not to look at bin Laden's political demands...

"What he has been demanding—for instance, the right of Muslim countries to their own resources [*I.e.* the right to fair prices for their oil]—is on the lips of almost every ordinary Muslim on the street in those countries. And, thanks to Al Jazeera, which has been exposing the corrupt elites of countries like Saudi Arabia, which have sold themselves to US corporate interests, it is even happening in the populations of those client states." (pp. A20-1)

And in *India Abroad* for August 3rd, 2007 the famed Catholic theologian Hans Kung, a German, is interviewed about Islam. He remarks:

"The policies of President [George W.] Bush, unfortunately, make it look as if the conflict of civilizations cannot be escaped. September 11 has to be condemned. But at the same time, one has to ask why these crimes have been committed. I think it is because of the role of the United States in the Middle East...If we want peace we have to come to the dialogue and not think we can resolve things by military means. We should never get away with using hostile images of Islam." (p.A22)

Whether or not you agree with Bilgrami and Kung, these two greatly dissimilar thinkers, what they speak of should be taken seriously and considered with care before we say that it's religion that's the incendiary factor in the Middle East. It's also revealing that an atheist should condemn the world's Harrises as moral morons. The latter for sure shows there's no unanimity among the godless and so no presumption in favor of sweet harmony were religion to vanish.

A friend of mine posed me this question: "[W]ould poverty-stricken, oppressed Buddhists do [the things militant Muslims are doing]?" Probably not. But we should take into account the very different characters of the peoples who became, respectively, Buddhists and Muslims. If the Arabs were religiously something other than Muslims, can we assert confidently that there'd be no Arab terrorists?

Look at the Arabs' history: at the tribalism, the fierceness, the intolerance, and the misogyny that they (along with the Afghanis) exhibited long before the time of the Prophet. The religion he passed on to them was one appropriate for such a

stubborn and combative people, letting those traits serve a religion and be gentled by that to the extent the believers were willing to have it so. Buddhism would never have caught on among
them. Islam was a civilizing agency that could counter the cen-
trality of clan connections, family self-interest, and harsh traditions sternly adhered to. Islam made social justice and equality
into important considerations.

And let's not forget that the new religion bloomed rapidly
into one of history's greatest civilizations, as Muslims moved to
the fore in the sciences and the arts.

What are the real factors precipitating the militants' acts
now? Are they for the most part acting selflessly as Muslims for
what they see as right? Or are they behaving angrily as frustrated
Arabs eager for vengeance and power? Can we say how much of
it is the former and not the latter?

Yes, some Muslims elsewhere, such as in Pakistan, are demanding the installation of repressive regimes and provoking
discontent and violence. But would they do so if the Arab militants didn"t? Do we know? And these, too, are relatively few, and
their activism, too, isn't independent of disturbed local conditions. The allegiance of most Muslims is still very much up for
grabs, and what will decide their patterns of behavior remains to
be seen.

We repeatedly tell the world that we believe in being good
neighbors and behaving justly and compassionately. If we acted
with any consistency as though we did believe in that, then at
the least it'd be harder for terrorists to recruit people to take up
arms against us. We might even make friends instead of enemies.
When I was a child half a century and more ago, Westerners
didn't hate Islam and weren't hated by Muslims. We might think
about why that was and what has gone wrong.

Harris theorizes about what more should be done to the Muslim world to secure our safety: "Whether such societies have to
be democratic is not at all clear. [Fareed] Zakaria has persuasively
argued that the transition from tyranny to liberalism is unlikely to
be accomplished by plebiscite. It seems all but certain that some

form of benign dictatorship will generally be necessary to bridge the gap....The means of imposition are necessarily crude: they amount to economic isolation, military intervention (whether open or covert), or some combination of both." (pp.150-1) Apparently his wishful thinking is such that he has learned nothing from our destruction of Iraq and its awful consequences. We did the kinds of things he wants us to do also when we returned the Shah to power in Iran and helped him stay there, which only turned Iran into a most dangerous enemy to us. The tactics he recommends, arrogant and contradictory to our ideals, are the same ones that got us into the straits we're in now.

How can he miss recognizing that what the Muslim peoples of the Middle East want from us, first and foremost, is that we *stop* telling them what to believe and how to live and which governmental institutions to have and who their leaders should be? If we persist in intervening massively and "crudely" in their affairs, that won't augur well for our future tranquility. It's far easier to bring about calamitous situations in that region than to re-make its peoples on our terms.

I'd say: Let the more moderate Muslim states of the world, such as Jordan, Turkey, Indonesia, Malaysia, and Egypt, do the mediating. Let them take the lead in bringing about cooperation in the Middle East and averting the proliferation of nuclear and biological weapons among Muslim nations, since they have as much to lose from disintegrating conditions there as anyone has; let's support and assist them as they do so, by all means taking advantage of the good offices of the United Nations. And let's be prepared to make large adjustments to globalization and corporate advertising that'll show good will to Muslim peoples who don't care to have our culture and ways imposed on them, just as we don't want theirs imposed on us.

III

Harris quotes suras including 9:73 and 9:123 of the Qur'an, which command war against "the unbelievers and the hypocrites" and against "the infidels who dwell around you," as evinc-

ing a warlike spirit in Islam. (p.32) He quotes sura 4:74-8, which
promises a better existence for those who die fighting for God.
(pp.33-4) It's important to realize that these suras, and in fact all
of the Qur'an, address the conditions of a time when Muhammad and his followers were beset and warred against because of
their religion and when their future safety and freedom of worship were in the balance. It's an error to generalize the meanings
of these suras so as to make them advocate perpetual worldwide
conquest or unconditional enmity to non-Muslims. Muslims who
are good people have never done so.

And why is it with Islamist extremists and not with decent
Muslims that Harris wishes to agree about Islam?

The above was already my opinion when I caught on television part of a talk by the scholar of religions Karen Armstrong.
Armstrong isn't a Muslim but knows much about Islam. She said
that Qur'anic commands to fight such parties as "the unbelievers," "the infidels," and "the hypocrites" referred to particular
groups known among the Muslims of that time by those desig-
nations, not to all non-Muslims in all times. She compared this
with the references in Margaret Thatcher's England to one faction of Tories as "the wets" (meaning they were weak) and to
another in John Major's day as "the bastards." The terms were
specific, not general.

Armstrong noted also that each time the Qur'an praises fighting for Allah it goes on to say that peace and forgiveness are better. She mentioned that Muhammad's enemies and persecutors
later became his friends, something I've always kept in view.

Harris: "The reality that the West currently enjoys far more
wealth and temporal power than any nation under Islam is viewed
by devout Muslims as a diabolical perversity, and this situation
will always stand as an open invitation to jihad." (p.32) Which
"devout Muslims" have those tendencies? None but the fanatical, of course. We don't know the percentage. If we assume it's
a high one, plainly we're saying there can be no peace between
the West and Muslims. Is that really something we want to take
for granted?

In India there's a Hindu heritage group called the Harmilap Sampraday, which has stood out for being well-intentioned and actively benevolent toward Muslims in a society where mistrust and ill will between Muslims and Hindus is more the rule. So impressed was one Muslim businessman with this that he built the Harmilaps a temple to show his appreciation and gratitude! Muslims don't regularly build places of worship for those who pray to idols, needless to add. It seems he did the most dramatic thing he could think of to reward their allorance. We can only wonder what *else* Muslims might be wont to do if their neighbors treated them so lovingly. I guess we'll never know unless others try it.

Harris: "Is Islam compatible with a civil society? Is it possible to believe what you must believe to be a good Muslim, to have military and economic power, and to not pose an unconscionable threat to the civil societies of others? I believe that the answer to this question is no." (pp.151-2) If the answer is no, it becomes awkward to explain how countries such as Turkey, Egypt, Malaysia, and Indonesia have managed to do it, the last of these being the largest Muslim society there is.

But Harris defines his terms as he chooses here: "What constitutes a civil society? At a minimum, it is a place where ideas of all kinds can be criticized without the risk of physical violence." (p.150) Realistically, there's nowhere on the planet that you won't suffer legal or extralegal consequences for behaving imprudently. If in the United States of the 1950s you publicly criticized the government's treatment of Communist party members or praised other Marxists, you were within your legal rights but might nevertheless lose your friends, your job, and your career. If you seem very friendly to Islam in America today, it's unlikely to do you any good.

Meanwhile, the far larger portion of the Muslim population of Indonesia is tolerant of unorthodoxy, even to the extent of Muslims worshiping trees and Hindu deities. No one prevents that or discommodes those who do it. It's probable that today heterodox Muslims are safer in Indonesia than *any* Muslims are in America. And if you or I conspicuously worshiped trees in America, we might meet with disapproval and social isolation. For sure we'd be under fire from Harris! So let's not be too categorical in speaking of what people are free to do, where.

IV

You probably noticed above that Harris picked up on the concept of *jihad* as though it were a synonym for mayhem. I'm looking at an online article from Washingtonpost.com, published by the Washington Foreign Post Service, for September 22, 2003, p.A10. It's titled "Islam Attracting Many Survivors of Rwanda Genocide; Jihad is Taught as 'Struggle to Heal.'" I'll give you a few quotes from it:

"While Western governments worry that the growth of Islam carries with it the danger of militancy, there are few signs of militant Islam in Rwanda."

"It wasn't the kind of jihad that has been in the news since September 11, 2001. There were no references to Osama bin Laden, the World Trade Center or suicide bombers. Instead there was only talk of April 6, 1994, the first day of the state-sponsored genocide in which ethnic Hutu extremists killed 800,000 minority Tutsis and Hutu moderates."

"'We have our own jihad, and that is our war against ignorance between Hutu and Tutsi,' said Saleh Habimana, the head mufti of Rwanda. 'Our jihad is to start respecting each other and living as Rwandans and Muslims.'"

"Since the genocide, Rwandans have converted to Islam in huge numbers. Muslims now make up 14 percent of the 8.2 million people here in Africa's most Catholic nation, twice as many as before the killings began."

"Many converts say they chose Islam because of the role that some Catholic and Protestant leaders played in the genocide..."

"In contrast, many Muslim leaders and families are being honored for protecting and hiding those who were fleeing."

One day I heard a story on National Public Radio about a Muslim Rwandan who admitted a Tutsi woman to his house when a mob was chasing her, then stood in his doorway and told her pursuers they couldn't have her. They went away. But that's only the real world, not Harrisland.

We should be aware that the great allors of India have never condemned Islam and that some of them were raised in it. Ramakrishna and Baba Lokenath studied Islam and became Muslims—not exclusively or permanently, but so as to experience the religion thoroughly. If it were all executions and subjugation and honor killings, they'd have opposed it in the name of God and humanity. They praised it instead.

V

While pondering these things I was on a local bus along with a half-dozen Muslim college students, young women who dressed in jeans and jackets but wore head scarves. From their faces I'd guess they were Malaysian. What most impressed me about them, once I decided to observe them, was how innocent and light-hearted they seemed. Those are qualities that open into greater spiritual receptivity. By American standards they were young for their undergraduate years—not childish but agreeably childlike.

I asked myself what distinguishes these religious young women from their American counterparts, female students who, while they may have had some religion in their upbringing, are living secular lives? I think the answer is that the latter would've been involved in sexual activity and relationships since their early teens, would've been exposed constantly to ultra-worldly entertainment, and would've been raised in a society that encourages self-centeredness and acquisitiveness. Young people in such circumstances often, I believe, can't be happy without having a specific reason for the happiness, since their culture has made happiness conditional upon getting what one wants.

That means they can't be happy usually or for long at a time. The Muslim women were raised in a society that emphasizes dutiful living, that discourages greed and self-centeredness, and that postpones and limits sexual conduct. They weren't hurried into adult concerns and responsibilities and anxieties while still children. The effect of all that is that they're less prone to being psychologically damaged and burdened.

I'd say that we who are part of the American culture, were we inclined to, could learn some valuable lessons from Muslim cultures, things that many Americans of a century ago knew but that've been lost in the coarsening caused by wars and in the welter of advertising, entertainment, celebrity-worship, celebration of sensuality, and unrestricted personal ambition, which has also reduced what religion has tended to mean to us as individuals.

I think of these softly laughing, companionable young Muslim women, who had a smile for me and who plainly hated no one. To rationalists they're enemies of reason and civil society.

I think of a very tall Egyptian graduate student who was a fellow employee of mine, the proud father of two small children, who is warmly at east with Americans. To rationalists he's an enemy of reason and civil society.

I think of a pregnant and glowing young Muslim wife, sitting at a picnic and amiably comparing notes on religion with an intellectual young Catholic woman. To rationalists she's an enemy of reason and civil society.

I think of that woman's husband, who wrote a heartbroken letter to the student newspaper of his university after the events of 9/11/2001, expressing his shock and dismay that Muslims could've done such things. He undoubtedly knew many Muslims, and he hadn't found them to be enemies of reason and civil society.

I think of the young Muslim woman I wrote about in Against Fundamentalism, who so radiated an inner beauty that the young American women she worked with adjusted their accustomed ways so she'd be comfortable spending time with them away from work. To rationalists she's an enemy of reason and civil society.

I think of the local Muslim women in the town where I live who've been profiled and interviewed in the news, and of how mature and good-humored and practical-minded, and downright *sane* they are. And I wish for the sake of everyone that rationalists could achieve an equal degree of good mental health.

I don't want to see these benign people caught in a vise between the foolishness of contending extremist groups, for and against religion.

Rationality surely requires that we try to resolve the mutual antagonism between the West and a small but rapidly growing percentage of the Muslim world. The writings of Dennett, Dawkins, Hitchens, and Harris can only exacerbate it. They're confrontational, uncompromising, and implicitly scornful of religious people and how they relate to life.

I'd say that trying to persuade the world's billion-and-a-third Muslims to choose between ourselves and their violent co-religionists by attacking their religion and trying to foster atheism worldwide has to rate as the dumbest survival strategy imaginable. Why would anyone even consider it? The people who come up with these notions are lost in their own heads.

We're being told by some that it's impossible to live in this world with Muslims. For the sake of perspective we should keep in mind that we were being told the identical thing about Marxists a generation ago. People are people first, and no one is unconditionally anything.

VI

The assumption in the West is that *we're* rational and the Muslim world is irrational. I have to wonder about our rationality. We who are Americans should observe how we've behaved till now toward Muslims. We don't seem to realize what we've done. It has been reminiscent of our treatment of our own native "Indians." Some examples:

- The forces of our secular Pakistani ally Yahya Khan killed a staggering number of citizens of Bangladesh—as many as three million—in an attempt to keep that province from gaining its independence. His military carried out that massacre with weapons it had earlier attained from the United States government, which makes it hard to

argue that it was no concern of ours. And we did nothing
to bring an end to it, although our own struggle for independence is never far from our minds. Today we scarcely
remember what happened in Bangladesh. If "all men are
created equal," what about those people, nearly all of
them Muslims? Why did we see them as expendable?

- We put the Shah back on his throne at a time when Iran
was trying to establish democracy, and we helped him to
remain there as a dictator for another quarter of a century, thus violating the human rights of the Iranian people. Then we were puzzled when it turned out that quite a
few of them didn't like us. (How could anyone be against
us, when we stand for wonderful things like freedom and
democracy?)

- We gave moral and material support to Saddam Hussein
when he attacked Iran, because we feared a militant Islamist contagion in the region and the political influence of
Ayatollah Khomeini. And so we encouraged and contrib-
uted to a needless war that went on for eight years and
took another million Muslim lives.

It appears to me that *most* Muslims have long been surprisingly forbearing and forgiving toward us. Maybe we should think
a little more about that.

There's something dreadfully wrong when we believe that
the killing of four thousand Americans by terrorists is a hideous crime while the killing of four *million* Muslims through the
scheming or the depraved indifference of Americans is a trivial-
ity. Where is reason when such evaluations appear and go un-
challenged, as they have among us?

Following, then, is an

OPEN LETTER TO SAM HARRIS:

Sir,

When you and your associates accuse the Muslims who are
living in our midst of irrationality and enmity to civil society,
do you give any thought to what you're risking, not for your-

selves but for them, most of them innocent people? Anyone can see that terrorism in Western nations will grow. Anyone can see that the wider population's anger and suspicion toward resident Muslims will expand as it does. As that happens, the danger must rise drastically for those millions of Western Muslims, who are helpless and at the mercy of all of us.

You can envision the horrible scenes as well as I can: the mobs' faces distorted by panic and hate, demagogues demanding vengeance, frenzied surges of armed people through quiet streets, police standing by or joining in, Muslims struck down on the sidewalks, their homes and mosques invaded or burned with them inside, their children clubbed to death.... We can't say that we in the West haven't seen it before. A holocaust with Muslims as its victims is not only possible but increasingly probable.

If you truly want reason to reign in human affairs, you'll do whatever you can to prevent such an outcome and do nothing that could precipitate it. That requires that you opt for reasonableness and not for rationalism. Rationalism can't co-exist with open-mindedness and good will, and reasonableness can't exist without them.

If we apply good will and reason, it should be apparent to us that what's desirable is a friendship offensive launched preponderantly by ourselves but carried through jointly by Westerners and Muslims worldwide, a movement that's active at every level from the governmental to that of the humblest citizens. It'd take high purpose and exceptional leadership to make it a reality. Instead of looking for ways to find fault with Muslims, we could be occupying ourselves with how to bring that about and with it a better life for many Millions of Muslims.

Such a convergence would be an inversion of earlier history, a reversal of the Crusader mentality. Both the religious and the secular could participate in it on behalf of their love of humanity.

That may never happen. If it does, it may be too late and too little. We may be too steeped in rage, fear, and passivity to attempt it.

But what that we begin today can better befriend the future?

NINE

THE MIRACULOUS

I

Are there miracles? Some of us know there are. Others think they know there aren't.

Dawkins: "David Hume's pithy test for a miracle comes irresistibly to mind: 'No testimony is sufficient to establish a miracle, unless the testimony be of such a kind, that its falsehood would be more miraculous than the fact which it endeavors to establish.'" (p.91) Can Dawkins give an example of a miracle testimony to the falsehood of which would be more miraculous than its truth? It's an empty category, I'd say, put forth as a witticism or rhetorical flourish by Hume. Dawkins, having the sort of mind that he does, wants to make it a Dogma of Science.

What are miracles? For here and now I'll define them as developments that violate the supposed laws of nature in a way that appears to be purposeful and either revelatory of something higher or of benefit to someone's health or safety or spiritual well-being.

Either miracles occur or they don't. I can't see any way to know which it is except by investigating. Above all we should study recent and contemporary accounts of miracles, as they're easiest to confirm or disconfirm.

Dawkins: "On the face of it mass visions, such as the report that seventy thousand pilgrims at Fatima in Portugal in 1917 saw the sun 'tear itself from the heavens and come crashing down upon the multitude', are harder to write off [than are miracles experienced solely by individuals]. It is not easy to explain how seventy thousand people could share the same hallucination. But it is even harder to accept that it really happened without the rest of the world, outside Fatima, seeing it too—and not just seeing it, but feeling it as the catastrophic destruction of the solar system, including acceleration of forces sufficient to hurl everybody into space." (p.91) Well, of course no one is saying that the sun in fact moved toward the earth.

He can't dismiss the matter that way. He resorts to a ruse, deflecting people from the main point. The main point is not that what was witnessed can't have literally been so, but that he has no naturalistic explanation for it or for the several other major Marian apparitions.

Dawkins was right when he used the word "vision" for what occurred. When seventy thousand people see the same phenomenon *and* that's accompanied by purported divine messages which the children who deliver them couldn't have thought up, then something is doing on that bids fair to be called miraculous.

It wouldn't be believable to say that everyone present was suffering from a brain disorder and that they all happened to have the same symptom of it at the same time. And Dawkins' expression "hallucination" is ill-considered. When a fantastic scene created through special effects is shown us on a computer or television or cinema screen so that persons with normal perceptual equipment all get the same impression of what's occurring when they watch it, we call it an illusion, not a hallucination. The same goes for seventy thousand people who unanimously view something that couldn't be veridical.

Clearly the special effects technology of 1917 was incapable of producing such a spectacle. So what did produce it? You and I and Dawkins can't say, at least for now. One thing that that means is that rationalism hasn't closed the deal.

I have before me an article on present-day miracles from a very down-to-earth source: the *Newsweek* of May 1, 2000. The first account is that of a young woman named Bernadette McKenzie, who at the age of twelve found herself physically unable to walk or even stand because of a condition called a tethered spinal cord. A group of nuns was praying for her recovery, which medical science said couldn't happen. One day she prayed, saying she'd be contented with whatever God chose for her but asking that *if* she'd ever walk again her favorite song be the next one on the radio. Right away her favorite song was played. She was so thrilled at this apparent promise of healing that she ran downstairs to tell her...Oops.

Now, what are we to make of that? Does anyone really think that the *Newsweek* reporters let themselves be bamboozled, that they didn't check with the doctors and the specialists and the neighbors, that this was a scam or a result of medical carelessness? But let's acknowledge that collusion for the sake of a good story is a possibility. The only way to know is to look into it. Has anyone done that?

In his book The Demon-Haunted World, cited in the second chapter, Carl Sagan attempted to debunk the claims of miracle healings at the shrine of Lourdes. He wrote: "The spontaneous remission rate of all cancers, lumped together, is estimated to be something between one in ten thousand and one in a hundred thousand. If no more than 5 percent of those who come to Lourdes were there to treat their cancers, there should have been something between 50 and 500 'miraculous' cures of cancer alone. Since only three of the attested 65 [it's now 67] cures are of cancer, the rate of spontaneous remission at Lourdes seems to be lower than if the victims had just stayed home." (p.233) Once again, the rationalist mind at work. He overlooked two factors that bear upon his conclusion.

One is that these cures occurred not just anywhere nor at just any time, but in one location and on the occasion of the pilgrim undergoing the procedure there. The other is that many more cures took place there than are, as he put it, "attested." That's because the Catholic church is exceedingly cautious about what it accepts as an official cure, not wishing to be shown up as wrong. If there's the least doubt or incompleteness of documentation in the case from beginning to end, or if the cure isn't instantaneous, that case isn't "attested."

And what of the great majority of Lourdes cures, which aren't of cancer? What would Sagan have said, for example, about the case of Marie Bire', who was blind because of withered optic nerves? She regained her sight, becoming able to read the finest print, although an examination of her eyes established that her optic nerves remained withered, making her sightedness a medical "impossibility"?

Dennett, Dawkins, Hitchens, and Harris make no mention of Lourdes in their books, which is probably shrewd of them.

II

There are people whose lives feature very strange events, and sometimes this has to do with religion and the miraculous. I've been one of them; and I know, and know of, others.

As for those of us to whom that applies, I don't at all believe that our exposure to the extraordinary makes us extraordinary or better persons or more favorites of God than are the rest of us; what causes it to happen, I don't know. It'd be interesting, as well as scientific, to examine such claims and such persons and see what correlates with what.

The episodes that I'm about to discuss are true. It'd be self-defeating to advocate true religion and yet lie on its behalf, because doing the latter would negate doing the former.

I'll begin with what happened to someone else in my presence. In 2000 I had the opportunity to spend a few days with two people in Western Pennsylvania who are close to Sri Sri Ravi Shankar (see the chapter on higher humanity). The two are unrelated and are rather different as personalities, but they're Caucasian, native-born Americans. Both are bright and autonomous and self-assured. The man is gay and was then in his thirties. (The charge that religious people are anti-gay, besides missing the fact that quite a few of them *are* gay, overlooks that the highest of religious persons, the allors, expect of gays only what they expect of straights, not that they become straight.) The woman was in her late forties or early fifties and is a prosperous small businesswoman with a husband and a son. They were working together, volunteering for Sri Sri's Art of Living Foundation.

During the time we spent together, the three of us paid a visit to the Sri Venkateshwara temple in Monroeville, Pennsylvania. While we were there, the woman prayed to the god's idol and, while doing so, uttered a stream of language in what sounded to me as though it could be Sanskrit (which she doesn't know).

Over lunch the man teased her about being "the only Hindu in Pennsylvania who speaks in tongues." She told us that the deity had said to her, "I'm going to give you *everything*." She thought that phrase to mean that she'd be effectually attuned to the conscious energy that's understood by Hindus to comprise *everything*, or in other words that she'd attain the oneness with *everything*—and so with God—that she seeks. I agree with her interpretation, as *everything* is a concept having resonance within a Hindu context. When, for example, the great nineteenth century allor Ramakrishna tearfully asked the goddess Kali, whom he worshiped, whether she was cruel, as some had told him, the answer that he heard was "I am *everything*."

Rationalists are sure to say that this woman was somehow a trifle deranged. I think not. Having spent several days in her company and knowing how she lives and behaves with family and others, I'd say that she's strikingly healthy of mind and that she manages her responsibilities quite ably and lives in a relaxed but vigorous way. The whole time she was with the man and me, she was calm, cheerful, and fully responsive to us and to what was going on. When she was worshiping and uttering the words in question she did so softly and without emotion. From all indications she wasn't disturbed by what happened or preoccupied afterwards with thinking about it.

(Rationalists avoid such people and such situations because they don't want to believe in their existence and what it says about life. And that guarantees that they know less about such matters than many simple and unschooled people do, while wishing to believe that they know everything there is to know about them. This is irrational.)

What should be made of the woman's experience and ones like it? Investigation into such events would let us better decide that.

III

I want now to recount to you some of the evidently miraculous events that I've experienced. (I've already told, in the chapter on faith, about one in which a prayer was answered before I could deliver it.)

The Lancaster Miracle(s)

In the summer after my sophomore year at college, I accompanied my parents to Europe. This was disorienting to me, and I developed a morbid religiosity. That was compounded by a considerable inferiority complex and a great lack of self-confidence that I'd had all my life.

I felt that after graduating I should join the Mennonites, whom I took to be very serious about religion. I was attracted to them partly because I saw pacifism, a commitment of theirs, as required of me (though not necessarily of everyone). This had to do with an inexplicable feeling of guilt that I had. The Mennonites I wanted to join weren't the Amish or the Old Order ones who dress in the manner of several centuries ago and forgo electricity, but modern ones who nevertheless are strict and in some ways unworldly. With my very limited knowledge of religion and my assumption from Bible verses that there could be no salvation except through Christianity, there seemed to me to be no alternative to this course.

My parents, who had raised me in a moderate Protestantism, were concerned at this but gamely went along with it, saying I had to do what I believed right. My plan was to go to Lancaster, Pennsylvania, and there establish contact with Mennonites, many of whom lived in the vicinity. I didn't speak in advance to anyone there about my intention. To do so would've embarrassed me and made me feel trapped by my resolution.

I had in truth very mixed feelings. I was fascinated by politics, something that I now felt I must put behind me. And while I tried to find moving the writings of Menno Simons, for whom the Mennonites are named, to a fair extent I didn't. So I was going to undertake something that I wasn't truly up for. Yet, distorted though it was, this did represent to me the delivering over of my will to God.

It would've been practical for me to approach some Mennonite congregation or organization beforehand, of course. They could've helped me to find employment, for one thing. Instead, showing my ambivalence, I checked into a very cheap hotel in Lancaster—later I moved into a nicer one at my parents' urging and with their financial help—and read the want ads each day, walking about from place to place as I hunted for work. Once I was working, I told myself, I could visit a Mennonite church with timing that suited me and without being dependent on, or owing something to, the first people I fell in with.

I wasn't hired, being "overqualified and under-skilled," as an employment agency told me. After several weeks of trying and feeling isolated and foolish, I gave up the project. With relief I decided to go to graduate school in philosophy in the fall, as I was happily able to do.

Thereafter my religious fixation gradually diminished. And my weeks in Lancaster, as you can appreciate, loomed in my memory as self-humiliating, unrealistic, and an indicator of how capable I was of messing up.

In the early spring of 1975, a dozen years after my Lancaster venture, my life took another turn. I had dedicated myself to working further in philosophy, on my own, while I held a shelving job in an academic library at Cornell. But now came the bizarre episode that I described in the second chapter of my book <u>Plato</u>. There's no need to go into the details here; suffice it to say that I suddenly had to question that philosophical thinking

could be taken at face value. With philosophy no longer an op-
tion, I was drifting, though I wasn't miserable and wasn't feeling
desperate for something to occupy my time.

A friend suggested I look into a motivational course offered
around the country and parts of the world, that was then called
Silva Mind Control and is now called the Silva Method. He had
heard that through it one could put oneself more in charge of
oneself and that it could even cause favorable things to happen
for one. The course, as I learned when I inquired into it, teaches
people how to enter an alpha brain wave state at will through
deep relaxation, and it provides training in the acquiring of very
positive attitudes and creative uses of imagination, even giving
rise to psychic abilities. It can be used, I read, to "program" oneself to change one's characteristics and one's circumstances for
the better. This very much seized my interest.

So I signed up for the June 7-10, 1975 course in New York
City. On June 6th I took a bus there, found the Silva headquarters which in those days was at 6 E. 39th Street in Manhattan, and
went to find the closest hotel.

I walked to the corner of 39th and Madison and looked around.
A block away, at Madison and 38th, stood a large, imposing, and
handsome hotel. There couldn't be a more perfect location for
me.

But down the right-hand side of the building stretched letters that spelled out HOTEL LANCASTER. And instead of
turning right, toward it, I turned left. The name Lancaster could
only seem to me a bad omen. I couldn't go in there, despite the
convenience! So I headed off, looking for another hotel.

However, dark clouds had been following me all the way from
the Port Authority bus terminal. I had kept an eye on them. Unmistakably a storm was impending, and there wasn't much time
before there'd be a deluge. I had an umbrella along, but I didn't
want to walk through a great downpour if I didn't have to.

Finally, with the storm close and no other hotel in sight, I
had to make up my mind what to do. Wasn't it silly for me to
make so much of a name? To preserve my self-respect by be-

ing practical rather than superstitious, I reversed direction and made for the shelter of the Lancaster.

As I was signing the register, having just missed the start of the rain, I could see through the open door that drops were bouncing high off the pavement.

The next four days—sometimes emotionally trying, sometimes delightful—proved to be one of the most formative and memorable experiences I've known. I can't think of them without joy. At that time a lot of bad stuff left me: the great bulk of the inferiority feeling and the self-dislike simply went and stayed gone. It was a fresh beginning. (I can't say that everyone there responded as I did, as reactions varied; generally, though, people appeared to be pleased.)

If Mind Control didn't represent the very highest level of spiritual understanding, it was nevertheless superior in that regard to most of what we're exposed to in America; of that I was and am convinced. For me it was a brightening of life and a step well ahead of what had been.

I saw irresistibly that my Silva adventure could be recognized now as the response to my having earlier sought, however weakly, to make myself available to God by going to Lancaster. The intention and not the outcome had been credited, I thought. While that earlier time had been a negative one for me, what I was given twelve years later was altogether positive. It was the opposite of the grim resignation that had been the mood of my sojourn in Lancaster.

It had taken a fortuitous storm to drive me into the Lancaster Hotel to keep my unsuspected date with the higher. Were the storm and the name of the hotel coincidences? I didn't, and don't, think so.

The hotel was a building I really liked. I stayed in it thereafter on repeated trips to the city, mostly for attendance at the same Silva course, which graduates can repeat for free, and for other Silva courses and functions. You could get a room for as little as eleven dollars a night in the Lancaster then, and it'd be clean. The building had towers and was fancy and irregular in ways that tickled me. The rooms offered differing sizes, shapes, and feels. The furniture was worn. One ashtray was from a defunct hotel, the McAlpin, I recall.

The Lancaster has since undergone remodeling and standardization and has become immensely more expensive, predictably; presently it's the Jolly Madison Towers, part of the Jolly hotel chain.

For years I was always able to get a room there, and I never reserved one. One time I checked in and the desk man said there was *one* room available—that a reservation had been canceled and he didn't know why he had saved it. (I thought *I* knew why!)

That's not all. One day I was visiting my mother in Pennsylvania and was hanging up my jacket when I noticed what was written on the wooden hanger. That was: "Midston House, Madison at 38th Street." Midston House I had never heard of, but the address was that of the Lancaster. So I asked my mother what Midston House was, and she said it was a residential hotel in Manhattan where my late father had lived before she married him.

Subsequently I looked at my father's reels of home movies and found footage of what was to me the Lancaster and to him Midston House, with an arrow inked onto the film that pointed to his room. The room had a round bathroom window, of which there weren't very many; with the assistance of what he had said and a hotel maid, I was able to locate that room, and I stayed in it several times.

Now, tell me, what would the odds have to be against my coming upon a Hotel Lancaster at a turning point in my life, when the name Lancaster was so significant to me?

What would the odds have to be against a storm arriving just then and forcing me into that hotel?

What would the odds have to be against my father having lived in that same hotel? It was all rather astonishing.

I reflected on that and asked myself: What must be the case about this world if such a thing can happen? It'd seem the causality of those events must've been operating well before my birth.

It'd seem, in fact, that the material factors that rationalists think are determinative in life must be mere playthings for forces that are spiritual or fateful.

Let me add this, incidental though it might be. At the time of my Silva course the big hit song was "Love Will Keep Us Together," performed by The Captain and Tenille. Thereafter, hearing that song inevitably made me think of Mind control and the love that I experienced through it. It was part of my extended experience of the course. Another thing that recalled Mind Control to me was a framed poster of a New York scene at night that I came across, which recognizably includes the Hotel Lancaster. After several moves, that picture had ended up in my storage space, miles from where I then lived; but a few months ago I was there and decided to bring it to my apartment. As I was boarding the bus with it, the driver's radio was on. It was playing "Love Will Keep us Together."

IV

A Three-Times-in-One-Day Miracle

One morning, two years after I took the Silva course, I visited a spiritual bookstore in Ithaca, New York, where I lived. I found a book that looked interesting and, since it was inexpensive, decided I could buy another as well. There was one about the great guru Ramana Maharshi, whom I had never heard of till then. (See the chapter on higher humanity.) His picture, showing him as an elderly man with a moustache and beard, was on the cover. I opened the book to several pages at random and found a quote that spoke to something that was on my mind; so I bought it.

That afternoon I was poking around in the stacks of Cornell's Olin Library, looking over books about spiritual figures. I ran across Paul Brunton's <u>A</u> <u>Search</u> <u>in</u> <u>Secret</u> <u>India</u> and read a little in it. It seemed Brunton found, as he had hoped to, a spiritual teacher of the greatest type. He used a title rather than a name to refer to him. I skimmed ahead and saw a picture of the teacher. It was Ramana Maharshi. I thought that was a funny thing: twice in one day.

Late that afternoon I paid a call on a spiritual-minded family I was friendly with. Their seventeen-year-old daughter was seated at the kitchen table. She was somewhat psychic. Talking with her and whoever else was present, I sat down beside her. She glanced at me and her eyes went wide and she said "Wow!" I asked her what was up, and she said she had seen another face superimposed over mine. This one had white hair and a moustache... I had a pretty good idea whose face she had seen. The next time I visited I brought along the book with Ramana's picture on the cover, and she confirmed that his was the one.

A few months after that—it was in the summer of 1977—I went to India and visited Ramana Maharshi's ashram. He had passed on in 1950, but his influence remains strong there.

I was never able to develop a feeling of devotion to him, but at times I could feel—and can—that he's deep within me. It seems we have business together, for which I'm glad.

V

A Miraculous Response to a Letter

As my interest in spiritual life grew in the years just after my Silva course, I read about and then visited Swami Muktananda Paramahansa, from Ganeshpuri, India, at his ashram in upstate New York. At that time the swami was very highly regarded by many people. After his death a number of disturbing things about him were revealed by former devotees of his. I don't believe now that he was a sadguru, though from what I observed and have read I do think he had some capabilities that were out of the ordinary. Such power as he displayed to help people spiritually I'd guess was effected through the higher influence of his own late guru, who was pretty surely an allor: Swami Nityananda, also of Ganeshpuri. What happened for me in this instance I've been prone to attribute to him.

One thing I knew about "Baba" Muktananda was that he didn't like me. He made that evident right away and consistently. At the time I had no idea why. I was there in all sincerity. Later I realized that it was probably the result of my having shaved my head, grown a moustache and goatee, and begun wearing red shirts. This followed upon the surge of new confidence that I obtained after attending Mind Control and was a way of reminding myself of it and trying to expand it. I wouldn't have believed that he could be so superficial as to base his assessment of me on that.

Some time after visiting "Baba" I was feeling frustrated at my failure, as I saw it, to progress spiritually. I wrote him a letter in which I dramatically asked for a breaking down of walls. Quite a while later I received a reply, in which he said to get my emotions under control, repeat the mantra, and always remember the Lord in my heart. It seemed to me not much better than a form letter.

However, the evening that I received it I went to a film on campus. It was "THX1138." The film depicted an under-the-earth civilization that was futuristic and repressive. Life in it was completely regulated, everyone's emotions and sex drives suppressed with drugs.

Everywhere in it were electronic booths, in which a bearded face with a turban could be spoken to for the sake of the people's morale. The mechanical figure first asked what was troubling its visitors. A moment later it asked, "Can you be more specific?" After a few moments, during which visitors could unburden themselves, it recited reassuringly, "You are a true believer." The lead character finally vomited in one such booth, unable to accept the falseness and manipulation any longer.

So, as I realized, there was a guru—an artificial one, or a parody of one—in this film, which was relevant to my situation. The lead character, moreover, looked a little like me, or so I thought, and stood out by having a shaved head like mine.

As the story continued, the lead character finally became determined to escape this hideous and absurd society (which could be a metaphor), although everyone had been told that the above-ground world was uninhabitable. Watching, I was absolutely convinced that he'd be apprehended or killed, that there was no way out for him.

In the final moments he was climbing hand over hand out of
the mechanized realm to freedom (which is what I was trying to
do, in my own way). A robotic guard was in pursuit and gaining
on him. But suddenly the guard stopped and announced loudly
that its budget allocation for this apprehension was exhausted. It
ordered the man to surrender and then, amazingly, *started climbing down!* The man succeeded in reaching the top and found himself in a world of sunlight, flying birds, and wild nature—a good
symbol of deliverance!

I felt, as perhaps you'll understand, that I had been awarded a
very specific promise in answer to my letter, at least for the long
term. And I did and do see the message as miraculous.

VI

A Miracle as Art

In August of 1995 I had cellulitis of the right foot. The foot
was swollen and badly discolored. The medications given me
weren't working, and when I arrived in the emergency room
of Tompkins Community Hospital in Ithaca, the doctor was
puzzled and was even speculating about AIDS as a possibility. I
knew it couldn't be AIDS, but if the infection weren't brought
under control I was in danger of losing the leg.

I had brought along with me to the hospital a copy of the
great Hindu epic the Ramayana, the Tulasidasa version. As I'd
be out of action for a time, it was an opportunity to finish reading this Medieval book that I I had purchased and begun reading in India. It may be spiritually meritorious to read, but it's
slow going by contemporary standards. I made some headway
through it during the days that followed.

Additional meds worked, and I was recovering. A physician friend of mine saw my name on the list of new patients and
stopped by my room during her rounds. Knowing that I liked
Indian things, she said that before I left I should look out in the
hall at the Indian mural that was there. Art wasn't an aspect of
the Indian scene that held much interest for me, and I promptly
forgot what she had said.

Shortly before I was to check out, my doctor friend stopped by again. She said to be *sure* to look at the Indian mural. So, once I was clothed, I stepped out into the hall. There, right beside the door of my room, was a painting called "Sitaram," which showed Rama and Sita, the divine couple from The Ramayana, at home in their forest exile. While I was in bed reading about their trials, they were right there keeping an eye on mine! The mural had been donated to the hospital by a doctor, by then deceased, whose name was Apu Sitaram.

I can't begin to guess what the chances are that a hospital in upstate New York would have a picture of Hindu deities in its hallway, let alone that they'd be the very deities that I was paying mind to in the nearest room.

VII

I well remember these things, but I don't expect anyone else would recall the details sufficiently to vouch for them. Others, of course, have had similar experiences. Why haven't all of us? I don't know, but people's attitudes toward them may have something to do with it. They've come to me unbidden but never unwelcome. Those whose worldviews exclude such phenomena may be unknowingly fending them off. But it's important to recognize that one doesn't approach the higher for such "presents," only for heightening. If the "presents" come they'll be, depending on how we take them, either a blessing or a temptation to look at life the wrong way.

On the basis of my experiences, what might one be inclined to think? Perhaps that all features of our world exist only relative to the higher. If that's so, then it may be that there's no inevitable causal necessity to the things that occur within time and space.

Science may one day apply itself to that idea. If it's found to be true, it'll put in shadow everything we've learned about our world till now.

Ten

The Uses of Imagination

I

As religion is beyonding, practicing it means moving past the assumption that what's most familiar to everyone—the material world—is all there is. The purpose of religion is to get in touch with the best of what's beyond us: the higher.

Imaginativeness is invaluable for beyonding. Being imaginative, devotional, and receptive at the same time can make real to our minds what we haven't outwardly experienced.

Rationalists will say that by doing this we come to believe in things that aren't real. But if imagination can be an alternative to the real, it also can be an interface with it and a segue to it in ways that most people don't know of and that any scientist should.

Being imaginative is is the opposite of what rationalists do, which is to shrink reality to the dimensions of their own preconceptions.

In this chapter I want to tell you about my experiences with people for whom imaginativeness and openness to additional possibilities combine into a way of life.

Years ago I visited New York City a number of times to repeat the four -day Basic Lecture Series of what's now the Silva Method and was then Silva Mind Control. What led up to that I've discussed in the chapter on miracles. From those trips I got more opportunity to learn how to be positive, hopeful, and relieved of cares.

I loved the course as I've loved no group association of mine. Most of what was sorriest in me disappeared after my first time there. Thereafter I was a freer person, and I've remained one.

The Silva techniques also are used to reach specific goals: to stop smoking, stop drinking, lose weight, get organized, etc. It's very practical as well as being fun and an adventure.

The system owes its being to the recognition that what we imagine in the requisite way, subjective though it is, can influence objective things: that we can concentrate on a desideratum and sometimes cause it to be manifested in the world. If that seems unbelievable, you might take the course and see, or at least talk at some length with someone who has taken it. With millions of graduates, such persons can't be hard to meet.

Let me add that I have no monetary or other connection with the Silva Method organization or with anyone connected to it. And I last took the course over twenty years ago. If you choose to take it, the gain won't be mine.

I can't guarantee that everyone who takes it will get the boost from it that I did. A few disliked it. Some thought it a grand time but then went home and forgot it. Others gave it a good go for a while but gradually drifted away or went on to something else. It may be that in most cases what's achieved in it is of short duration, as people return to old mental habits once back in their old surroundings. Not everyone can get to the graduate meetings, which raise morale and reward continuing effort. I wish I had been able to. I seldom use any of the techniques today; but I've remembered, and I try to live, the spirit behind them.

This is no cult. Far from it being difficult to get out of the Silva community, I had trouble remaining on the mailing list. The organization makes no demands on you. The whole idea is to better enable you to creatively decide and accomplish things for yourself, while cults want you to be dependent on them.

The course has been with us since 1966. The road to it began in the '50s when Laredo electrical engineer Jose Silva was able to improve his daughters' performances in school by hypnotizing them and, as he related, one started answering his questions before he asked them.

I should add that there's nothing wholly new about the Silva system. Dr. Joseph Murphy in his book The Power of Your Subconscious Mind, published in the 1920s (various editions), provides much of the intellectual and technical groundwork of what was to emerge independently of him as Mind Control. Whether it originated even with him, or still earlier, I don't know.

I'm not going to describe the course in full, but this should give you a taste of it. For anyone who wants more information, there's plenty on the Internet, both what's posted by the Silva people and comments on it by graduates and others. I've seen in the latter testimony much that's at least moderately pro and nothing that's gravely con: no charges of fraud, of sexual exploitation, of enslavement, of arms stockpiling, etc.

II

That first day of my first course, June 7th, 1975, I entered a large room with rows of chairs and people milling about. I gave my name to two women who sat at a table. One was a handsome 51-year-old veteran actress from the TV soaps named June Graham (now Spencer), who was the instructor. She had red hair and brown eyes and a dramatic flair, as well as a fieriness that she had tamed pretty well, but never completely.

Present were several dozen adults, young and middle aged. In many of us surely was a hope of finding real happiness that we usually won't acknowledge to ourselves; we withhold it because we don't want to be unsophisticated in the eyes of the world and are afraid of being disappointed.

June introduced herself and gave the introductory material, explaining how the course had been developed and what its theory is. The theory is that deep relaxation can put you into an alpha brainwave state (we're normally in beta), in which you can visualize what you want to see realized; and if you do it right, that may come about, though you must be clear on what it is that you want. This process, combined with a very positive attitude and good will toward everyone, tends to break down the mental barriers between people and make you a bit psychic.

After lecturing for some time—to get us restless and ready to escape, she explained—June had us close our eyes. She talked us through an exercise in which we physically relaxed ourselves, something otherwise not always easy for people who've been negotiating Manhattan. She had us do some visualizing, picturing our ideal place of relaxation, which could be anywhere we wished.

Always the emphasis was on what works for you as an individual. Your "points of reference" are your own. When you're relaxed and at ease yet attentive to your aim, she said, you find your way for yourself.

It's sometimes alleged that what the Silva Method teaches is self-hypnotism. Its proponents deny this and assert that studies of the brain waves show it to be something else. You are, at any rate, at your own effect and not that of the instructor. As June recited in a soothing voice, "This is mind control, your own *self-mind control*; it is for your benefit, you desire it, and it is so."

Further relaxing and visualizing sessions followed, interspersed with more information, many anecdotes, and answers to people's questions. The pace seemed unhurried, and humor and curiosity were always in the air.

We each constructed a mental laboratory in which we could use chemicals and devices to work on projects such a healing people and improving their circumstances and our own. It was a way of focusing our energy.

All of this was instrumental to the work we were learning to do. What Jose Silva was trying for is a world of independent and freely cooperating problem-solving psychic activists: "To qualify as humans we must take part in humanitarian activities." We could decide for ourselves what to do; others might join in but no one could dictate.

At one point we (physically) handled a collection of metals, mentally going inside each one and feeling what it was like. Then some of us related what we had felt. This was done to help us be more inwardly responsive to what's around us.

We contemplated an imaginary elevator whose door slid down from the top. Inside we were to find a counselor who could advise us. We didn't choose the person: as the door descended we'd "see" who it was. I "saw" upswept white hair and, being politically-minded, decided it was Andrew Jackson. We could ask our counselors questions and get advice from them. I'd say it was a method for de-personalizing our intuition, becoming one step removed from it so we wouldn't so readily discard its deliverances through self-doubt. For the same reason we also learned to "put on" the head of anyone—say, Einstein—so as to "hear" practical answers to what we wanted to know for our work.

Later we got a second counselor. I don't recall who mine was. Andy stayed around for a bit, then gave way to a young woman named Eileen with whom I had just been discussing Mind Control. I still ask her to help me find Christmas and birthday gifts for people, and, by chance or not, I've had a knack for that.

There's a glass-of-water technique, involving drinking half a glassful at bedtime after posing a yes-or-no question, then drinking the rest in the morning whether or not the answer had come in a dream. You should have the answer within seventy-two hours. It might be in a headline you've noticed, an overheard remark, a sudden thought—anything. I used this technique in my room in the Lancaster the night after learning it. It seems to me that what I asked was when I'd change as a result of what I was learning. The next morning, the first words out of June's mouth were, "Things happen when you're ready." As soon as she said it, I had an uncanny recognition, extending to conviction, that those words had come as my answer.

The prime technique is called Mirror of the Mind. The idea is that you relax completely, taking and releasing breaths while counting down from ten to one, then picture a screen in front of you: not on your eyelids but a short distance away. On that you visualize the outcome you want. You do so for at least twenty seconds. You continue to visualize it whenever you "go to your level" or in other words enter that relaxed and stable state of mind. That should be for at least fifteen minutes per day. This process is called programming. "To program is to think a thing over and over."

Does this work? I've heard and read more than a little testimony that it can. When I returned home I had the wish to be more social and outgoing. Specifically, I wanted to be asked to parties. That hadn't been happening, so the odds weren't good. After several days of my programming for that, a co-worker came by and invited me to a party. Coincidence? I can't be sure. The invitation may have been influenced by my more upbeat persona. Other things I programmed for, such as finding a girlfriend, didn't materialize.

In the minutes before the start of a 1982 workshop I attended at Mind Control, a woman in front of me told the woman beside her that she had programmed that her paycheck would double; subsequently, she said, the company began issuing paychecks half as frequently, so that each was twice as large. She added that she hoped her fellow employees didn't trace this innovation to her, since it was highly unpopular! I still chuckle over that. A Mind Control instructor would probably say she didn't believe she deserved the additional money. But her effort did bring a result, apparently!

For our own peace of mind and inner freedom, as well as out of good will, we can imaginatively reconcile ourselves with someone we've been at odds with, June told us: "It's very hard to get angry at someone you've been walking through the woods with at your level."

(Some of her remarks I wrote down as she made them, and those I'm putting in quotes.)

It might be asked why it is that people who worry all the time—thus thinking a thing over and over—so often find their fears unrealized. I think the Silva people would say it's because the worried thoughts are "in beta," while it's alpha that makes the repetitions effectual. Someone who's tense and anxious isn't programming properly, even if vividly "seeing" a dreaded situation.

III

After I came back from Mind Control, two young women who were co-workers of mine went to New York and took the course on my recommendation. They stayed in the home of friends of one of them in Queens and drove into Manhattan. On the course's final day, Kathy had trouble finding a parking space and let Peggy out so she could go in. Peggy explained why Kathy was late, and the instructor led everyone in sending her energy. Kathy later told the class what happened. As she walked along the streets after parking, she related, everyone she passed said hello or smiled at her. This is *New York City* we're talking about! She said that one especially sour-looking man walked all the way past her, then turned around and said, "Good morning!" And it may be that that's what it's like to have a roomful of people vibing you. I hope one day we'll all know first-hand.

I've stuttered since I was five years old, and my efforts to program against the stutter appeared only to worsen it. Peggy offered to also program that it end. One day, for about a minute, while I was having lunch and had been thinking about other things, I had a sensation that I couldn't stutter, that whatever I said would come out freely. That was nothing I imagined. It was powerful while it lasted. It's what other people implicitly have all the time, but I hadn't had it in many years. I afterwards asked Peggy if she had been programming at that time to remove my stutter, and she confirmed that she had been, sitting out on the ag quad under a tree.

Peggy decided before long that the whole Silva process was too repetitive and artificial for her, and she gave it up. I can only speculate whether, if she had continued to program for a minute or so each day for several weeks, my stutter would've yielded. Even if so, it also might not have stayed gone once she finally stopped.

What are the limits on what should be programmed for? June warned us not to try to control other people, especially for selfish reasons. She told a story of research scientists who had successfully used visualization to stop children from wetting their beds, and who then decided to see if the children's bed-wetting could be started again, as well; the experiment had to be halted, she said, when a thirty-five-year-old scientist started wetting his bed. Did that happen? I've no idea.

She also told us the reportedly true case of a Mind Control graduate who wanted a certain woman to marry him. He programmed this repeatedly by picturing the two of them walking arm-in-arm into the apartment building where he lived. She married someone else. Then she and her husband moved into the programmer's building, where coming face to face with them was painful for him. One day he ran into the woman on the street when almost home. She must've been in an exuberant mood, because she took his arm and marched jauntily into the building with him. And while this was going on it occurred to him that it was exactly what he had visualized! But it had come about literally instead of in the figurative way in which he had meant it to.

So trying to control the minds of others wouldn't work and could only backfire, we were told. Then again, I met a graduate in one of the courses who boasted to me that he used programming successfully to give people headaches!

Someone who became a friend because she also had taken the Silva course told me this supposedly true story as a cautionary tale against trying too hard: A Catholic woman very much wanted to find a husband, so she got a little statue of the appropriate patron saint and would pray to it enthusiastically several times each day. Nothing happened. She prayed still more fervently. Nothing happened. This went on for months, with no sign of a break. Finally one day she entered the room, saw the statue, and was overcome with fury. She snatched it up and hurled it out the window! A moment later there was a knock on the door. A man was standing there holding the statue and rubbing his head where it had hit him. She married him.

The point is that she got what she wanted the instant she stopped pushing it with her will. It's necessary to get out of your own way and *let* the desired thing come about, my friend said, rather than trying to force it to; so I should do the programming, then forget about it till the next time.

A woman quoted June Graham to me as having said "Inanimate objects—ha!" I take her point. June told us that the pay phone in the classroom (which had been fixed to accept only outgoing calls, so as not to disturb the class) was a special one that had its own personality and purposes. If you didn't reach your party, it'd hold onto your coin for you and drop it into the slot once the party was available, she said. I don't know about that, but I can tell you what happened the sole time I used it. I was going to call someone I had met in one of the classes so we could arrange to get together. When a break came, I waited while another man made a call and failed to reach his party. His dime (what a call cost in those days) didn't come back when he hung up. Thinking he was dealing with an ordinary pay phone, he pounded on it a couple of times, then returned to his seat. I, by contrast, looked upon the phone with friendship and a touch of reverence; it pleased and intrigued me to think that it could be somehow alive. As I stepped up to it, it dropped a dime into the slot. I took the dime over and gave it to the other man. Then, as I went up to the phone again, it dropped *another* dime, and I got a free call. Inanimate objects—ha!

I can imagine what rationalists would say about *that*. But I think we'd all be happier if we were more open to the magic and mystery and whimsy of life, including even the wacky notion that a pay phone can befriend us! Especially when it appears that it can.

June had a good sense of what was going on in the class and was apparently able to affect it in ways of her own. I remember something that happened several times. She'd stop and ask, "Who has the headache?" A sheepish hand would go up. June would return to her lecturing, and a few minutes later she'd look at the person and ask, "How's the headache?" "Gone!"

June told us a tale about someone who was programming to re-grow an arm. Anyplace else we'd have laughed, I'm sure, but in that setting we just found it interesting and wondered if that could work? I think she knew that where "That's impossible" doesn't crop up, life is better, and more *is* possible.

She also didn't hesitate to inject her own views and some minor practices into the course, which occasioned friction with Silva headquarters in Laredo. "I don't believe in reincarnation," she quipped, "but then, I didn't believe in it the last time, either." She said her favorite religion was Daoism, which probably wasn't true of anyone else in the room. She remarked that even Jesus wasn't above having a bad temper. My hunch is that she did these things to let us see that when we were relaxed and in good spirits we didn't tense up or bridle at them, as we might've done otherwise.

She recommended we protect a person or a building by mentally putting a white light around it; another instructor told me that Laredo had ordered her to desist from that. June told us in a confidential tone that Jose was "stuck." I think Jose wanted to prevent the course from evolving past his control.

June eventually left—definitely Mind Control's loss!—and started a course of her own called "Let Go and Live," which is defunct now. It didn't duplicate Mind Control but allowed her to go her own way without interference.

IV

In one class I went up to her on a break and asked about a woman Cornell student who was missing. I showed her a clipping. She looked at the student's picture, then closed her eyes for a few moments. Then she asked me if the woman were religious? I said I had no idea. She remarked that the woman had had a mystical experience. She took a piece of my notebook paper and drew a standing figure with arms outstretched, as though in flight. I then mentioned that there was speculation she might've jumped into one of the gorges, a method of suicide that Cornell students called "gorging out." June contemplated that for a little while and said, "That may be it." Long afterwards, when the student's body was found in Cascadilla Gorge, I mailed June the article and included her sketch of the tragically flying figure.

The final day of the course, just before graduation, we performed health diagnoses at a distance. June joked that now was the part of the course when she gave her body to the class. We closed our eyes and scanned her. We agreed she looked healthy. One woman detected what she thought was a scar from breast cancer surgery. June said that was accurate.

We then sat together in pairs. Each of us had in mind an acquaintance who was ill or disabled. We took turns describing the condition of the person our partner was thinking of, as we "saw" it. Then we'd change partners and do it again. We were sometimes very accurate, sometimes not. The case I recall was that of a man who appeared to me to be entirely gray, though I couldn't find one location that was impacted more than another. My partner then told me that the man had terminal cancer which had spread throughout his body, and that he was receiving chemotherapy that had turned his skin gray.

Afterwards June pointed out to us that we hadn't looked at these unwell people judgmentally, hadn't faulted them for what was wrong with them. She said we could take the same attitude toward those who behave badly. No one, she said, *wants* to be angry, hostile, or cruel. We take on those traits because we're afraid. "Once you get in the habit of seeing everyone as they'd like to be," she remarked, "you live in the most wonderful and generous of worlds."

She addeded, "I changed my attitude toward tyrants, and I haven't met one since."

Doing cases, she said—reading the health of persons and sending them energy—would bring good things to us as well as to them.

We were able to feel ourselves, in that classroom of people, as a community in which we were in harmony and no one was holding out. People were reading each others' thoughts like old couples. We'd report identical images occurring to us at the same moment. We rarely know such occasions. Small wonder I kept going back for more!

The only drawback I found to the course is one's own negativity, which can be brought out by all the positive surroundings. The sole time it strongly got to me was in one of the later classes I attended. During the final day I began to feel discontented. I should've known better, but this was emotional. I thought that I must've gotten all from Mind Control than I could. I was sad and felt helpless.

I decided to leave at the next break, because I knew that this negativity could radiate to others in the room. Then suddenly that mood was gone and I was euphoric and at peace. What happened? I think June must've spotted the black cloud over me and zapped it, as she did the headaches. I sailed through that afternoon, then stayed around after most had gone and chatted for some time with June and a few others from the class. That day brought the lowest low and the highest high that I experienced in Mind Control.

I took a short course in psychic healing with Jose Silva one time, also in Manhattan. I wasn't very good at what he taught, and I no longer recall much about it. Jose himself has stayed with me, though. He was a short and broad man with a manner of quiet confidence. Even up close he never crowded you with personality or authority. He seemed someone you'd want to spend time with.

He wasn't charismatic; he came across as altogether genuine and spoke to the class as he might've spoken to three or four guests in his living room. When we got a break, he didn't but stayed in front of the room answering questions for whoever came up. I very much liked him and thought him completely real and trustworthy.

Jose was thought heretical enough by some that there was an attempt at one time to excommunicate him from the Catholic church. It failed. He was a devout Catholic, and the course, especially in the early days, was often taught to and even by nuns, who were offered it for free.

I was in so many Mind Control classes and observed so much that I can't doubt that being imaginative, positive, loving, and physically relaxed can make us happy, intuitive, and sometimes psychic. It's a good thing—a grand thing—to realize. It lets us feel a solidarity with one another that we otherwise don't. Jose's dictum was that in alpha we all pray for each other and in beta we all prey *on* each other.

V

Some who are religious may contrast programming for a result, which expresses one's own will, with praying for it, which leaves it up to God's will. Jose saw the ability to program as God-given and perfectly natural and right. It doesn't seem to me that programing for an outcome is very different from going out and working for it or kneeling down and praying for it. In programming and (in separate instances) in praying, I've noticed that doing either tends to make you more accepting of whatever comes—more dispassionate about it. I consider that significant. I don't see praying and programming as opposites, and I'm not inclined to see them as incompatible.

I think of all the people who sit in churches on Sundays, trying to remain awake. I think of all the congregations that are passive even while singing. I wonder to myself how anyone can settle for that? If they can, it's only because they don't know there are alternatives.

I don't have to tell you that rationalists, if they ever took the Silva course and didn't sabotage themselves, would find their barren little world exploding into a charmed technicolor riot! I'm not looking for that to happen. But you never know what might.

Imagination has been employed in religion but rarely, it seems. Loyola devised religious exercises in which one would imagine in detail scenes from Jesus' life, such as his boyhood home. Some Hindu worshipers mentally assume roles from the youth of Krishna, becoming the Gopis, his neighbors, his friends, his mother, etc. Such activities take devotion higher.

There's much that could be accomplished in religion through what the Silva course (and, earlier, Joseph Murphy) taught. Some day, I hope, many people will find the incentive to experiment with it and to listen to those who accomplish the most with it.

A Silva class *feels* different than even an admirable religious service does, and I've pondered how that's so. I think the class's light-heartedness, the continuous good humor, the absence of any obligation to hold the same beliefs, and the real hope of change are the ingredients of the difference.

If we're able to bring to our quest for heightening that spirit of uncoerced love and freedom, if we can have the devotedness of true worship and also the relieving happiness of letting go of anxieties and accepting other people as they are, then, I believe, religions can make a quantum jump ahead.

ELEVEN

THE OBJECTIFYING OF RELIGION

I

I'd make an appeal here to religious people to recognize the subjective character, and therefore the mutual reconcilability, of the major religions. For the religions to oppose one another can only weaken the confidence and good will of their believers without resolving anything.

To say, "The beliefs of my religion are factually accurate though I can't prove it" is to permit rationalists to defeat you in argument. If we recognize those beliefs to be loftlore—to be justified by what our attending to them devotionally can accomplish for us—then your such beliefs and mine and everybody else's can be accepted as true in the truest sense.

Geneticist Francis Collins, of Human Genome Project fame, has written The Language of God: A Scientist Presents Evidence For Belief (New York, Free Press, 2006). A Christian, he thinks that the extreme unlikeliness of those conditions in the universe that render human life possible is congenial to a belief in God as creator. But isn't it perfectly conceivable that the improbability of human life may one day be dispelled, because the conditions that give rise to it will be accounted for in naturalistic terms in consequence of new discoveries? Can we say with any assurance that that won't happen?

I think it's a real weakness in Collins' position that what he believes about God is falsifiable, if only in principle. Do we want religion to be a gamble?

The Hindus who once worshiped their creator deity, Brahma (seldom worshiped nowadays), had no interest in the facts regarding the origins of the world. Their faith wasn't vulnerable to anything that science may disclose, or to any external factor whatever. Therefore, psychologically and spiritually, their position was impregnable, while Collins' isn't. They had no need for reservations or mental asterisks alongside what they believed, while he has.

Shouldn't religion set us free, not lock us into a cage constructed of necessities and impossibilities?

I'm not implying that Collins or others should abandon Christianity for the worship of Brahma. I mean that they should contemplate religious and scientific knowing and see that they're distinct, with fact coming *first* (through investigation) for science, and *last* (through transformative outcomes) for religion.

Collins: "What we cannot discover, through science alone, are the answers to the questions 'Why is there life anyway?' and 'Why am I here?'" (p.88) I'm not sure that's so. As I've said, I'd like science to interest itself in heightening and the higher. I'm not willing to restrict in advance what such an endeavor might accomplish.

Doing as scientists tend to do, many religious people view religious beliefs as objective—as factual claims—supposing that only the beliefs of a single religion, at most, can be the truth. Collins, good and honest-hearted as he is, realizes the unsatisfactoriness of that. Yet he can't avoid it because he's caught within the either/or model that factuality presents us with.

Collins: "Far too much has been said by Christians about the exclusive club they inhabit. Tolerance is a virtue: intolerance is a vice. I find it deeply disturbing when believers in one faith tradition dismiss the spiritual experiences of others. Regrettably, Christians seem particularly prone to do this." (p.225) But two pages later he writes this: "(I)f faith is not just a cultural practice, but rather a search for absolute truth, we must not go so far as to commit the logical fallacy of saying that all conflicting points of view are equally true. Monotheism and polytheism cannot both be right." (p.227)

Will he see that his latter statement *is* the exclusivism that his former statement deplores? He'd have tolerance be both a "virtue" and a "logical fallacy." That's confused thinking. And why must "absolute truth" be about facts rather than pertain to what's not less but more than factual?

For many contemporary Christians there's a dilemma, then. They want to assert that their tradition is true in a factual sense, which in practice means denying the truth of every other tradition; but the better people among them also want to embrace those of other religions, respect their autonomy, and be responsive toward their insights.

Let me tell you how to resolve the dilemma. Monotheists and polytheists alike have found their truth subjectively, by embodying such ideals as allorance, heightening, and wisdom. "Conflicting points of view" *can* be "equally true" when they bear equally healthy fruit. If we stop trying to say what's real—and how can we know the dimensions of that?—and start thinking about what changes us, we'll fare better.

Practicing one's religion doesn't entail falsifying others' religions in a "search for absolute truth" that takes place apart from our heightening. We know the higher, to the extent that we do, not from authority or from plausible conjecture but from the elevation and refinement of our own and others' minds and emotions.

Always it's a mistake to try to justify religious beliefs through objective factors. You can't rightify yourself by wrongifying others.

Is God the God of the Bible, or of the Qur'an, or of neither, or of both? If you have an experience of God, can you identify that experience as representing any of those? Better to go by the immediate than by the abstract, as what's immediate isn't problematic. People harm one another because of what they believe of God, not because of what they've experienced of God.

We must also be ready for our beliefs to change. They may give way to others that in part confirm and in part alter them. Infinintention is a necessity of life and of religion. What that's human has ever stayed still? If we absolutize our beliefs by factualizing them, we take a stand against our own evolution.

II

Let's reason—about your religion and others' religions.

Monotheist versions of the Deity are represented as zealous for the worship of themselves and violently opposed to the worship of other divinities or their idols. Herein is a dispute from of old. There are Jews and Muslims and Christians and Sikhs and Zoroastrians on one side and Hindus and Jains and Pagans and Buddhists and Daoists on the other. Can this disagreement justify religious intolerance?

If you think non-theistic religion is wrong, consider the supremely benign figures who've practiced Buddhism and been transported in spirit beyond our known limits. If you think the worship of idols is wrong, I can show you, from recent centuries, far more spiritual greatness in persons who've practiced idolatry than you can show me in persons who've condemned it. If we're practical, these things tell us what we have to know. Being intuitive can do so as well.

If you say it's a *fact* that God condemns idol worship, I ask you to prove it. And I don't think you can. It's one version of things, helpful or harmful depending on how you employ it. Employed best, it's loftlore, a feature of stories that you can contmplate devotionally, and has no bearing upon what happens to exist in the external world. Employed as fact, it opens the door to smugness and resentment and hatred and persecution—and not to anything good. If it's a spiritual truth, shouldn't believing it have spiritually elevating consequences? History witnesses that it doesn't.

As I mentioned in the chapter on the truest faith, I worship Hindu deities. If that's forbidden by God, how is it that I and countless people who do the same feel love for God through do-ing so? Theory mustn't be permitted to trump evidence, as it does for rationalists and fundamentalists.

The only evidence that we're viewing God in an acceptable way is that we're heightened. Not "what the Bible says" but what our experiences and the quality of our lives say should be deter-minative. If God wants to instruct or punish some of us for get-ting it wrong, how is it that we undergo spiritual growth instead? And how could our doing precisely that *not* be what God wants for us?

Christians who insist it's a fact that God's forgiveness is pos-sible only for those who believe in Jesus Christ should think further. The very atmosphere of the higher *is* forgiveness and healing and rebirth. The story of Jesus dramatizes and doesn't monopolize what can happen in people at large in relation to the higher. If non-Christians can undergo heightening, then the burden of proof is on Christian exclusivists that salvation means something that isn't heightening and that can't be attained by means of it.

What can we really say about God? What does God do? Do we know? We're right conventionally to attribute to God the out-of-the-way things that benefit us. But would it be cheating if higher beings of some sort hear our prayers and provide what we ask without taking credit for it? Can we say that that doesn't happen?

What I'm suggesting by asking this is that we have no knowl-edge that makes theists more spiritually right than non-theists.

I'm going to coin the word "Godding" here. To God is to act as we think of God as doing: not in the sense of humans ar-rogating authority to themselves and so "playing God," but in the sense of beings beyond ourselves rightly performing labors for us that we attribute to God.

How much of what we declare that God does is actually God-ding? Some? All? None? How do you know?

And if you can't say, how can you say that it's not only God but your tradition's version of God that does all these things?

III

Understanding religious beliefs as factual claims leads to further errors. They are: trying to corner people with facts on behalf of a religion, and trying to falsify other religions. All three of these infest another prominent Christian book: apologist Lee Strobel's The Case For Christ (Grand Rapids, Zondervan, 1998).

Religious commitments should be made freely and from inclination, so they can flourish and endure: *not* because one sees no alternative. Since the job of religion is to liberate, how can we employ it to enslave people in a worldview that doesn't appeal to them? And remember the old adage, "One convinced against his will / Is of the same opinion still."

Christians tell us that we have free will. But some of them threaten us with eternal damnation if we don't join them. Those who believe that threat *aren't* free to choose according to their true preference. What one does with a gun to one's head isn't done freely or because one is convinced of its inherent rightness. Strobel doesn't use the damnation tactic, but his recourse to factuality also constricts our inner freedom, and it's meant to.

There are no good religious choices that are made from fear, whether of damnation or of being objectively wrong. We should harken to our innermost feeling for higher ways, not let ourselves be pressured. If anything in this world deserves to be wholly voluntary, it's the selection and the practice of a religion. Religion should attract us only by being attractive.

Strobel aims to strengthen belief in the New Testament as objectively right by showing that the particulars it alludes to are true or at the very least not impossible. To do that, he carries skeptical questions to experts on the Bible and the ancient world.

He doesn't see it as a conflict of interest that all of these scholars are fundamentalists like himself and are therefore predisposed to see things his way. Other highly-regarded scholars might dispute some of their conclusions, but he doesn't inquire of them. He uses the metaphor of a legal trial for this process, with his chosen experts as his witnesses and the verdict to be the reader's, for or against the believability of the New Testament. But I've never heard of a trial in which only the defense was permitted to present evidence.

Strobel records that he said in the course of a discussion with one of his experts, "Okay, but you personally have faith that Jesus was resurrected..." (p.115) What factual claims such as that call for is proof, not faith. Absent the possibility of proof, they're loftlore or fanaticism.

Strobel's experts attest to the accuracy of some New Testament statements; they reveal, for example, that the little places like Bethlehem and Nazareth that it names have now been confirmed to have existed in Jesus' day, and that Roman governors did indeed require people to return to their places of birth to participate in a census. His notion is that the more correct details the New Testament is found to contain, the better it looks for what it says about Jesus' divinity and his miracles.

But think about that. If schemers were going to make up a tale about a messiah and induce later people to believe it, don't you reckon they'd include as many real places, persons, institutions, and events as they could, to invest it with verisimilitude? Why would they invent towns that pilgrims and inquirers wouldn't be able to visit or trace?

The Gospels and the apostles' letters, Strobel's experts state, were written close to the time of the events related in them: not generations after, as critics have thought. There remains debate as to that. And does it matter? The Bible as I see it—and I've read all of it—reads like an unabashed and artful mixture of history, folklore, and mythologizing. There were esoteric groups among the Jews, such as the prophet schools and later the Essenes and the Therapeutae, about whom we know only what they chose to reveal to the public. The ancient world tended to be secretive about the most important things it knew. (My second book, Plato, is about that.) If Jesus and his followers belonged to an already established esoteric tradition, their group might've produced a mixture of myth and fact, and it might've begun doing so immediately because that was its received way of comprehending and teaching.

Isn't that as possible as what Strobel says?

Strobel would like us to believe that the resurrection of Jesus must've occurred as fact if we're to explain the enthusiasm and the fearless expansion of the early church. But it's evident that the emphasis in the New Testament is on the activity of the Holy Spirit. So if the early members had inspiring and somewhat transformative spiritual experiences, that could've outweighed all else and been what prompted them to act as they did, no matter what had happened factually.

Isn't that so? Can he give us a reason for putting aside the idea?

One of the book's sections is titled "A Faith Buttressed By Facts." (p.52) It can be a thrill if the facts fall the way you want them to, but in religion a dependency on facts is crippling. Using facts to buttress faith is like using crutches to walk when you don't need them; over time you get so you can't walk without them. We've all read the news stories about an essuary turning up which contained what some think are Jesus' bones. That's a reminder how quickly and devastatingly a reliance on some cluster of facts could be punished by the unanticipated discovery of contrary facts.

Wouldn't you say so, if you think about it fairly?

Those who must have their faith with facts may end up with facts instead of faith, or with neither. Faith comes from insight, which comes from devotion and commitment. Faith is nullified when made contingent.

Why would a person of faith want to confirm scriptural accounts, anyway? Better to *dis*confirm them, so one's faith can't be weakened by uncertainty. The concern for historicity is just that—a concern. Religious life should lift us out of needless concerns such as that, while enabling us to handle unavoidable ones without worry. Whatever was should be fine with us.

It's aggression to misrepresent or make up facts. One of the people Strobel quotes told him, in conversing about the religions he had looked into, "Hinduism believed in all these crazy orgies that the gods would have..." (p.176) He's misinformed. No religion favors purity more than Hinduism or does more to help people treasure it. Several years ago some Christian group on the Internet claimed that the Hindu gods took drugs. This unscrupulousness and infighting indirectly reflect on the religions of those responsible for them.

Religion will be subjective or else be an excuse for indulging in intellectual dishonesty, untruthfulness, and fearfulness. Worship is subjectivity. If religion is subjective, then it needn't make God objective. And "not objective" doesn't translate as "unreal."

Because of that—because receptiveness and not factuality is the great catalyst in religion—theistic and non-theistic religionists can be in accord and still be faithful. And if they can be, they ought to be.

IV

What follows is an experiment. I want to treat the Christian understanding of God as consisting of factual claims, as Collins and Strobel and many Christians do, and see how able that understanding is to meet the questions that arise from it.

My first question is, Why is there a creation? Why would a deity bring into being a material world such as the one we find ourselves in? What's the good of it, the gain from it? We're usually told by Christians that God created us because he wanted human companionship, or else because he wanted worshipful service. Why would he? If we go by the Bible, he already had angelic company in great numbers, and that'd seem to be a more edifying type of company than ours.

More basically, how can God be perfect without being self-sufficient? How can he lack something and be God? Why would he need other beings?

And if you were God, would you create something like this world? Reportedly in heavenly worlds physicality and the difficulties and pains associated with it are absent. Why cause them to be, then?

If you ask this, you're likely to be told that we can't know the mind of God. But Christians are the last ones who should be arguing that way. By saying that God took birth as a human to let us know him, they're saying that God is intelligible to us, and moreover that he intends to be. So I repeat: Why the physical creation?

Perhaps they'll venture to say that something God wants can be accomplished through the physical. But that's so theoretical, and so unsupported by their scriptures, that we can't conclude anything about it.

The Christian thinker and visionary Rudolf Steiner said we've incarnated to divinize matter. Why should there be matter? And if there's some reason for it to be, why isn't it already divinized? I'm not insisting he's wrong, just asking if we can say he's right with any confidence?

Also, why does there exist in this world such ignorance of God and such widespread remoteness from divine ways? Now we'll be told: It's like that because man has free will and has chosen to disobey God. On p.43 Collins quotes C.S. Lewis, his favorite religious writer, as saying that it's nonsense to want God to both give us free will and deny it to us. But it's Lewis who's not talking sense here. Look at the people we say know God, the best and divinest humans. The presumption is that they both obey and have free will. So it must be possible for God to create humans who are free *and* voluntarily obedient. If he can do that in some instances, why can't he in all?

Say I'm a creator of beings. I can create you to be free, with either a high or a low capacity to appreciate your creator and love higher things. If it's with the low capacity that I create you, why should I blame and punish you for not having enough of what I gave you too little of?

Also, contrary to what theologians say, I have to doubt that the wicked *are* free. It seems to me that they're at the mercy of their appetites, warped valuations, and illusions, at least some of which they were born with. Aren't the people who are obedient the same ones whose hearts are turned to God? Then surely the answer to the problem of sin would've been for each of us to be confirmed from birth in devotion and attentive closeness to the higher, as some are. *Then* we could've made use of our free will without folly resulting.

If God created the world *ex nihilo,* then the way it is is the way he intended it to be, sin and all. People may not be pleased with that answer, but I don't see how they can get away from it.

Why is there sin? Why is there agony? Why are there such terrors and such miseries? "Recognize," writes Collins, "that a great deal of suffering is brought upon us by our own actions or those of others, and that in a world where humans practice free will, it is inevitable." (pp.231-2) But given a God who's omnipotent, omniscient, and omnipresent, it plainly *isn't* inevitable. As Collins himself writes, if God is "supernatural," "then He is not limited by natural laws." (p.81) And even if God lets you harm yourself with your free will, why should he let you harm others who haven't willed that harm? And what of all the suffering in the world that's *not* caused by humans, such as many diseases?

Collins: "Hard though it is to accept, a complete absence of suffering may not be in the best interest of our spiritual growth." (p.232) And what of suffering that ends rather than enlarging whatever belief the victim may have in God's providence?

Granting that suffering can yield spiritual growth, why should a loving and all-powerful God require hideous suffering, when he could provide the growth with little or none?

Everyone who attacks the Christian worldview demands to know how a God of love could impose eternal damnation, something even Hitler would've stopped short of? And there remains no defensible reply.

If everything that happens, including the worst things, is "God's will," as Christians often declare in consoling one another, what does that say about the free will they also say we have?

Is belief in Jesus Christ God's answer to sin? If so, why does that belief commend itself only to members of a single religion and not to everyone else equally, whether greatly or little? Is God truly so inefficient and so easily compromised in his work?

And if humanity is the intended product and beneficiary of the creation, why is there so much in it that's extraneous to the human? Why would nature take *billions* of years to disgorge man? Why should there have been dinosaurs dominating the planet for vastly longer than we've been on it? If *we're* the point, aren't *they* completely beside it? What did God have in mind in creating them?

And why are we humans existing amidst so many other forms of life? Why are there pigeons, bats, microbes, tse-tse flies? Why are we linked to all physical beings by DNA if we're essentially different from them? Why are there innumerable apparently lifeless planets, solar systems, galaxies? If it's all about *us,* what's *that* all about?

Moreover, if this world is a creation, why must it be God's? If God is perfect and the world very imperfect in a plethora of ways, how can they be, respectively, creator and creation?

I haven't heard and don't foresee any traditional Christian answers to these questions, only the repetitions of pat recitals.

Before people can call it a *fact* that we live in a creation of God's, I think they must at least explain the purpose of it and the reason for its imperfections. And if they can't, doesn't that call into question what they do profess to explain?

Yet all of these questions disappear for Christians who look upon their worldview as loftlore, seeing it as subjective and not necessarily as factual, while what can be experienced through their religion—such as heightening, allorance, devotionality, penitence, and the miraculous—remains, as much for them as for the literalists, if not more.

This necessitates a doubleness within the worshiper. The religion is to be taken as it presents itself, yet openness to facts in the world must not be obstructed by doing that.

I also want to challenge the way some Christians have tried to get the upper hand by representing any who disagree with them as unrepentant sinners and therefore as biased rather than rational. There are many penitent and holiness-loving members of other religions.

Exclusivism is far from rational and is purely a curse. Instead of drawing unbelievers, it gets their backs up.

V

I'm going to try my hand at a more intelligible account than the traditional Christian one of how things may *objectively* be in a general sense, going by what we already know about how they are.

I'm centering on the world's *aggregationality*. I don't ask that you take this as final, just that you give thought to it. I'm speculating, not delivering "teachings." Recognize, please, that I'm being tentative about this—and only about three-fourths serious.

And, as ever, what the facts are (assuming the true state of affairs can be grasped in those terms) makes no difference to true religion.

I'll say that this world is one expression of a totality that's expressed in endless ways and that simply *is*. The universes, the dimensions, the modes of being, the beings—all are *literally* infinite in number and variety. (When I think of the higher I have to think of it as imbued with infinity and universality, because nothing less is worthy of it or intuitively right for it, and this fits with that.)

We can call this view *allinclusivism*. It regards everything as ontologically and epistemologically prior to anything.

That means that the physical doesn't exist for a purpose. It exists because everything exists somewhere, unto infinity. It's the infinite that's the most real. Entities are and cease to be in one setting or another, while the same ones are, maybe always, in other settings.

What exists includes what's thought of as logically impossible. What can impossibility be but our confession that we don't see how something *could* be? And what has that inability of ours to do with what actually is? Perhaps an accordion fold of our conceptual capacity will at some time open out and we'll perceive to exist what we had always declared incapable of existence.

Therefore it's natural, and necessary, that the physical should exist, and its existence has nothing to do with whether or for whom it's desirable. For example, there can be both dinosaurs and humans, with neither a privileged type of being. The prime cause is not God's will but aggregationality.

This structuring of things means that there are realms in which there's no God, ones in which there's nothing but God in discrete forms, and ones in which God's being varies in what it's like. Our world is one of the ones in which God *sometimes* is. You can tell that from the fact that we aren't all forever encountering God. You can tell it also from the fact that some of our great religions are theistic while some aren't. For us, God is a possibility, not an inevitability.

If it's asked how God can be God and yet exist only sometimes and in some locations and in contradictory ways, I reply that what's primary isn't God but a state of things which sometimes manifests as God.

Collins: "The Big Bang cries out for a divine explanation. It forces the conclusion that nature had a defined beginning. I cannot see how nature could have created itself. Only a supernatural force that is outside of space and time could have done that." (p.67) That conjecture is invalidated if each is because all must be.

Scientists today are increasingly speculating about parallel universes, a multiplicity. If there's no sure evidence for that, there's even less evidence for a creator. Does the universe seem too complex and well- designed to have come about by chance? Maybe it didn't but also wasn't created. It is, if so, because elsewhere everything else is, and there's nothing that can not-be.

With heightening goes allorance, or being with *all*. That seems significant. This *all* isn't just all of the beings on earth but absolutely all beings everywhere. We can regard ourselves as either unique or "of our company'": that is, as in each case one apart or as in each case the aggregate represented from a particular angle as a being which is something in its own right. I'd say it's the latter view that better lets us relate ourselves to the higher and think in universal terms.

If God existed at all times in this universe, one consequence should be, I'd think, that we'd all both love God and have the same conception of God. Not only is that not the case, but it seems to me that what people love when they love God is really the higher (to which we attribute mystery, beauty, and regard for us), and their own potential for being heightened and so made free, fulfilled, and happy.

It could be that the higher is what (alone) pertains to all states of affairs, infinite though they are in their variety. How can we know? Yet perhaps one day we shall.

We don't find that one so loves God's personhood, however that's described, as to remain a theist on that account amid doubts. Likewise, people who were formerly devout Christians but who fell away and decided to join other religions weren't deterred from doing that by love of Jesus; what Jesus represents to them is also represented to them by other deities and by the higher and isn't unavailable to those outside theism.

I'd argue that allinclusivism may be the most believable version of how things objectively are. But whether it is or not, religious people don't need an objective account of higher things and can only put themselves into a quandary by chasing after one.

TWELVE

RELIGION AND SCIENCE

I

When an interviewer asked Charles Proteus Steinmetz (1865-1923) in what field he thought the greatest discovery would be made in the following fifty years, he replied: "...I think that the greatest discovery will be made along spiritual lines. Here is a force which history clearly shows has been the greatest power in the development of men and history. Yet we have been merely playing with it and have never seriously studied it as we have the physical forces. Some day people will learn that material things do not bring happiness and are of little use in making men and women *creative* and *powerful*. Then the scientists of the world will turn their laboratories over to the study of God and prayer and the spiritual forces which as yet have hardly been scratched. When that day comes, the world will see more advancement in one generation than it has in the past four." (Quoted in Conde', Bertha, What's Life About?, New York and London, Charles Scribner's Sons, 1930, pp.45-46, italics in original)

As I know rationalists will say I'm an outsider without an understanding of how scientists actually work and think, I'm leading off this final chapter with those words from someone who was not only a scientist but a scientific genius with few peers. I was almost through with this book's preparation when I happened across that quote, but it wasn't too late for it to register as a timely gift to me and so to you.

If Steinmetz was right, rationalism is irrational, its denigration of religion the loss of a great scientific opportunity. Think of that!

If the likes of Dawkins and Harris answer that he was less a real scientist than they, where are their scientific accomplishments to surmount or even rival his? He wasn't a theorist but someone who, without precedent, created lightning in a laboratory.

He was mistaken, of course, about scientific inquiry into prayer and God occurring within a half century of when he spoke. But he unarguably thought that it *should* occur; and he was always ahead of his time.

As for what he was proposing, it might or might not be identical to what I proposed in the first chapter: that scientists look into heightening, wisdom, and the miraculous, and that they attempt to engage the higher. To do these things they'll have to be willing to be changed, themselves, without setting a limit to how or how far. It's unclear if Steinmetz anticipated that; having read his biography, I think he was insightful and courageous enough to go along with it.

Through what procedures did he want scientists to study God? I don't think we can say. I'd speculate, based on the quote above, that he saw God not as a cosmic personality but as the highest natural force, one that has brought about a gradually accelerating historical growth of knowledge, infinintention, and appreciation of allorance. How might he have seen the Bible, the holy writ of his land and his ancestors? Perhaps as a coded way of talking about that.

(Steinmetz knew and may have been influenced by Hegel's depiction of history as the self-working-out of consciousness, in which, through its internal logic, each advance is at once affirmed, canceled, and absorbed into a more adequate whole (*Aufgehoben*).)

When a first-rate scientist like Steinmetz can regard religion as the key to our future, the rest of us can better recognize the reflexive anti-religiousness of rationalists as an un-critical-minded component of our contemporary scientific culture and not as one warranted by scientific principles.

II

Rationalists are tiresome. I think most people will catch on to that, the more we hear from them. Their one-sidedness chafes our sense of fair play and our regard for impartial inquiry. Their love of impossibilities sets up roadblocks to where we naturally wish to go. Great minds like that of Steinmetz don't behave so but awaken us to possibilities and stir our imaginations. They, and not people who want to improve the world by abolishing tolerance and respect, are the ones we can most intelligently entrust with helping us to design our planet's future.

I've a higher opinion of scientists in general than to believe that the majority of them want rationalists speaking for them or riding herd on them. That's why I distinguished in the foreword between the new, angry rationalists and sciists, the latter being persons of science who are neither religious nor anti-religious.

Particularly in view of the foreseeable social and political consequences of rationalism's belief that it has all the answers, I'd wager that most scientists will have none of it. Here's an

OPEN LETTER TO SCIISTS:

Respected Men and Women of Science,

I cordially invite you to speak your minds concerning an authoritarian danger that's issuing from the world of the sciences.

It's the rationalist view that to work in a science is to deny higher possibilities and that no disagreement with that by anyone, inside or outside of the sciences, is permissible. This is an acid eating through that greatest of scientific tools, empiricism.

To be true to itself, science can yield nothing to prejudice and wishful thinking. I therefore ask you to inform us on your own authority as scientists that rationalism isn't science but something alien to it that makes it wear blinders and rides piggyback on it.

I'd also encourage you to take a public stand unconditionally on behalf of our interlocking Western traditions of personal freedom, human rights, and democracy, because the overthrow of those traditions would rob science of its independence and its unconditional honesty.

-John Gibson

III

Religion approaches all that is subjectively, science objectively.

But science can learn how to explore subjectively and evolve that exploration toward the accumulation of objective data. Scientific research can't be complete until it does so.

Science at its best and religion at its best have an entente by virtue of the infinintention that both incorporate. They should make the most of it.

If we want better people in a better world, there must be more religion, not less. And it must be better, truer, higher religion. That calls for readying ourselves with our very greatest intelligence and passion, purifying our aims and perceptions, and going forward without letting distractions deter us.

Whoever wants to practice or study religion will have to know how to go about it. These are steps to beginning that:

- Decide what kind of religion you wish to attend to. If it's a non-theistic kind, read about it and if possible talk with someone who has made headway in it. In what you undertake, follow the guidance of an expert, preferably in person.
- For a theistic religion, find the object of worship that has the most appeal for you. That being should represent to your mind the higher and purity and allorance and should inspire you and capture your imagination with the mysterious beauty of its being. Pay no mind to what others think, as religion is the most personal and intimate activity there is.
- Develop devotionality. You can do so by means of worship. It may include wholehearted prayer, in which you praise the deity and encourage in yourself the desire to be changed for the better. It may also include ritual forms

of worship, which you can read about in the literature, and pilgrimages, however minor and local, to identify it in your mind with sweet experiences and make it the more precious to you.

- Worship at the same time or times each day, and be unhurried in it. Make it more important to you than the rest of what you'll be doing. See that its importance is in its filtering you into the higher and the higher into you.

- Read devotional and spiritual works from more than one tradition. Prefer them to entertainment. You'll gradually acquire a taste for them and develop a subtler mind, so that what you read will become more interesting and engrossing and edifying as you go along.

- Whatever tradition you adhere to, look into its recommended methods of contemplation, meditation, and/or yoga. But don't be afraid to try the methods of other traditions.

- Don't listen to those who want you to doubt. What matters isn't what you believe but what you're prepared to discover and adapt yourself to.

  Religion is about experiencing and being heightened, not about affirming debatable theses. Don't disbelieve. Don't believe. Be committed to your exploration of the higher.

- Be very aware of allors from various traditions, both earlier and contemporary, and hear them thankfully and thoughtfully.

- The *only* test of your rightness is the magnitude of your devotion and your desirousness of serving all.

- Remember that what you have to gain is real and enduring happiness and the truest relevance of yourself to everything else that is.

GLOSSARY

Allasease: all as ease, complete mental easiness and imperturb-
ability: the likely nature of the truest faith: the dissolving of
otherness in stable psychological comfort (Chapter Four)

Allinclusivism: the theory that everything exists because the nature of things is such that everything must exist, precluding a
divine or other creation (Chapter Eleven)

Allor: one who is for, disposed favorably toward, all without exception, as are pirs, saints, sadgurus, walis, sages, etc.: the
most morally outstanding and psychologically free humans
(Chapter One)

Allorance: the attitude and practice of being for all, as distinguished from giving preference to oneself and one's own kin
or kind or co-religionists (Chapter One)

Allorist: one who follows an allor, especially when the dedication
is more to the allor personally than to the allor's tradition or
recorded words (Chapter One)

Beyonding: religion understood as our intended surpassing of the
known limits of things in order to be heightened (Chapter
One)

Godding: possible performances by higher, so-called supernatural beings, that we attribute to God, such as intervening on our behalf (Chapter Eleven)

Heightening: the raising of a person to superior awareness and such humanly advanced behavior as compassion, purity, and competency; heightening is the purpose and work of true religion (Chapter One)

Higher, the: whatever is beyond the physical and psychological features of existence that we all know; presumably God or divine beings or heavenly worlds or states of being such as Nirvana, etc., or some or all of these (Chapter One)

Infinintention: in true religion and true science the refusal to limit with finality what can be, which affords us greater humility and intelligence that's unconstricted (Chapter One)

Introverse, the: subject matter of a probable future theory that the world and direct knowledge of situations can be discovered within oneself, as allors have said they do (Chapter One)

Loftlore: the tales, doctrinal beliefs, etc. of a religion understood as intended to contribute to our heightening rather than to describe a factual state of affairs (Chapter One)

Ongoer: "ghost," "deceased" yet consciously existing and active human or other formerly "living" being (Chapter Six)

Rarenaut: (future) scientific investigator of the rarefied, consciously purified human mind and its objects in exploration of the higher (Chapter One)

Sciist: rationalist of the earlier type, a scientific thinker who's
   distinguishable from the new rationalists by maintaining scientific tentativeness and not being hostile or triumphalistic
   toward religion (Foreword)